THE CORRESPONDENCE OF ROBERT BRIDGES AND W. B. YEATS

Also by Richard J. Finneran

W. B. Yeats, *John Sherman and Dhoya* (editor)
William Butler Yeats: The Byzantium Poems (editor)
The Prose Fiction of W. B. Yeats: the Search for 'those simple forms'
Letters of James Stephens (editor)
Anglo-Irish Literature: A Review of Research (editor and contributor)
Letters to W. B. Yeats (co-editor)

THE CORRESPONDENCE OF
ROBERT BRIDGES
AND
W. B. YEATS

EDITED BY

RICHARD J. FINNERAN

First published 1977 by
THE MACMILLAN PRESS LTD
London and Basingstoke
Associated companies in Delhi
Dublin Hong Kong Johannesburg Lagos Melbourne
New York Singapore Tokyo

British Library Cataloguing in Publication Data

Bridges, Robert
The correspondence of Robert Bridges and
W. B. Yeats

1. Bridges, Robert 2. Yeats, William Butler
3. Poets — Correspondence
I. Title II. Yeats, William Butler III. Finneran,
Richard J.
821'.8   PR4161.B6

ISBN 978-1-349-03156-6   ISBN 978-1-349-03154-2 (eBook)
                           DOI 10.1007/978-1-349-03154-2

Typeset in Great Britain by
SANTYPE INTERNATIONAL LTD
(COLDTYPE DIVISION)
Salisbury, Wiltshire

For Mary

Contents

List of Illustrations

Robert Bridges
1. An 1897 drawing by William Rothenstein. From *English Portraits* (1898)
2. An early photograph. From *The Bookman* (London), December, 1898
3. A 1912 photograph, the frontispiece to *Poetical Works* (1912)
4. Bridges as Poet Laureate. From the *Illustrated London News*, 26 July 1913

W. B. Yeats
5. November 1896 portrait by John Butler Yeats. First published in the *Literary Year-Book 1897*
6. An early photograph, from *The Outlook* (New York), 2 January 1904
7. An 1898 lithograph by William Rothenstein. Reproduced in *Liber Juniorum* (1899)
8. A 1908 photograph. From D. J. Gordon, *W. B. Yeats, Images of a Poet* (1961)

Preface and Acknowledgements

This edition contains the extant correspondence that I have been able to discover between Robert Bridges and W. B. Yeats: twenty-seven letters from Bridges and fifteen letters from Yeats. Also included is the single letter from Yeats to Mrs Robert Bridges. It is clear that not all the correspondence has survived, but I believe that this volume includes all but a few of the letters that passed between the two writers.

Eight of the Bridges letters have been previously published in full in *Letters to W. B. Yeats* (1977), ed. Richard J. Finneran, George M. Harper, and William M. Murphy; the remainder are published complete for the first time. Fourteen of the Yeats letters have previously appeared in Allan Wade's edition of *The Letters of W. B. Yeats* (1954), but Wade regularized the punctuation and spelling, made some small errors in transcription, and purposely omitted a name; the other Yeats letters are published for the first time.

In addition to these published versions, two different sets of transcriptions of the correspondence exist. At some point before the summer of 1952 an unidentified scholar (possibly Joseph Hone) transcribed all but two of the Bridges letters, then in the possession of Mrs W. B. Yeats. These typescripts are now in the library of Senator Michael B. Yeats. In the summer of 1952 Mrs Yeats returned the Bridges letters to the then Lord Bridges. He and his son (the present Lord Bridges) then transcribed the exchange of correspondence. One set of these typescripts is in the possession of the Bridges family; another set was presented to the Bodleian Library, Oxford, by Mr Simon Nowell-Smith in 1965. In 1971 Dr John Kelly discovered two further letters from Yeats to Bridges in the files of Longmans, Green & Co.; through the kindness of Mr Guest of that firm, these were returned to Lord Bridges. Transcriptions were made and added to the set in the family possession.

With one exception, the text of the letters is taken from the manuscripts in the possession of Lord Bridges. My aim has been to present the letters in the form in which they were written, and thus the term 'sic' does not appear. Occasional editorial interpolations are placed in square brackets. As indicated in the headnote, the Bridges letter of 15 June 1897 is reconstructed from a transcription and a printed source; the original is apparently lost.

Of my many debts, the most important are to Lord Bridges, who first suggested this edition and who gave permission for the use of his grandfather's material; to Senator Michael B. Yeats and the Oxford University Press for permission to use the Yeats material; and to Dr John Kelly, co-editor of the forthcoming Oxford University Press edition of the *Collected Letters of W. B. Yeats*, for providing transcriptions of the Yeats letters and for advice on their dating. I would also like to thank Mr Robert O. Bridges and Miss Anne Yeats for access to the respective libraries and for copies of materials. For other assistance I am grateful to Professor Mary M. FitzGerald, Mr Peter Kuch, Professor Jon Lanham, Mr D. S. Porter (Bodleian Library), Professor Ron Schuchard, and Professor Donald E. Stanford.

Newcomb College, Tulane University,   R.J.F.
New Orleans, Louisiana

Introduction

In the spring of 1896 J. W. Mackail brought to the attention of his friend Robert Bridges a volume entitled *Poems* (1895) by W. B. Yeats. Bridges proceeded to send Yeats a brief but admiring letter. He had to wait six months for a reply, and when it came it was unsigned; nevertheless, this exchange began a friendship between the future Poet Laureate of England and the first Nobel Prize winner from Ireland that was to endure until Bridges's death over three decades later.

Yeats must have been flattered to receive Bridges's praise, as by 1896 the older writer (some twenty years Yeats's senior) had established a secure reputation among those with a serious interest in literature. Two years earlier, for instance, the authoritative *Times* had commented that 'intelligent readers of contemporary poetry do not require to be told that Mr. Bridges is a first-rate workman and that his is an original mind'.[1] Moreover, Yeats surely had read the essay by his close friend Lionel Johnson in *The Century Guild Hobby Horse* for October 1891; although denying Bridges the 'final grace and grandeur' of poets like Arnold or Wordsworth, Johnson still described him as 'the most admirable in recent times'.[2] And Yeats also may have known Edward Dowden's flattering assessment in *The Fortnightly Review* for July 1894.[3] Indeed, in the notes to his *A Book of Irish Verse*, published in March 1895, Yeats had cited a lyric of Bridges as illustrating 'the rapture and precision of poetry'.[4]

Once established the relationship developed quickly, and in some ways the first few months of 1897 are its most significant period. As early as January Yeats told Lady Gregory of his intention, once he had obtained 'a little theatre somewhere in the suburbs to produce romantic drama', to include one of Bridges's plays (doubtless *The*

Return of Ulysses) in the repertoire.[5] In April Yeats included
Bridges's offer of his home as a kind of country retreat.
notes of poetry and of them alone', in a list of those writers
dedicated to 'the calling of what is personal and solitary to
the supreme seat of song'.[6] Yeats's visit to Bridges at
Yattendon on the last weekend of March, during which he
received detailed criticism of his *Poems*, was followed by
Bridges' offer of his home as a kind of country retreat.
Yeats's appreciative essay on 'Mr. Robert Bridges' in *The
Bookman* (reprinted in Appendix A) lead to Bridges's long
letter of 15 June, offering his views on Yeats's short fiction.
But then there seems to have been no further correspondence
for some two years; and in fact the relationship after this
period became one of scattered letters and infrequent
meetings, with only occasional episodes of greater
involvement.

The basic reasons why the friendship did not become
more intimate seem clear enough. Bridges, for instance, did
not share Yeats's interest in the revival on the stage of poetic
drama: 'I don't expect (or really wish) to see a play of mine
on the stage,' he wrote him in 1899.[7] The offer of the Manor
House in Yattendon as a place where Yeats could escape the
pressures of life in London was probably not taken up
because of the availability of Coole Park — Yeats spending
the first of his annual summer residences there a few months
after his visit to Bridges.[8] And although each writer quite
obviously admired much in the work of the other, there were
fundamental differences in background (Bridges a retired
medical doctor of independent means, Yeats lacking both
money and a university education), temperament (Bridges
avoiding literary politics in the seclusion of Yattendon, Yeats
busy with the founding of Societies in Dublin and London),
and aesthetics (Bridges a classicist characterized by restraint,
Yeats in the nineties a symbolist committed to the eternal).
A letter from Bridges to William Rothenstein on 2 June 1898
is representative of the tenor of the friendship: 'Yeats I
know. He has been here, and we want him again — he is a

true poet, and delightful company, but he is in great danger of fooling himself with Rosicrucianism and folk lore and erotical spiritualisms. It is just possible that he may recover – some of his work is of the very best, both poetry and prose.'[9]

Yeats did not of course 'recover', and for many years after 1897 the correspondence becomes sporadic, much of it concerning anthology rights for Yeats's poems. An exception occurs in 1901, when Yeats sent Bridges a lengthy description of his psaltery experiments with Florence Farr. He must have been disappointed with the response: 'I can't really imagine a recitation which I shd like as well as a good reading.' Some letters were exchanged in 1913 about Yeats's use of the expression 'four-fifths' in his Introduction to Tagore's *Gitanjali*; but again, Yeats must have been saddened when Bridges – now the Laureate – refused his invitation to join in the festivities honoring Wilfrid Scawen Blunt.

So it is not until 1915 that we find an extensive exchange of letters. Most of them concern two issues: the inclusion of Yeats's poems in Bridges's anthology *The Spirit of Man* (1916) and the textual corrections in them Bridges considered necessary; and Bridges's desire to enlist Yeats's aid in persuading Tagore to allow a rewriting of one of the *Gitanjali* poems for the anthology.[10] During this year also occurred the second and, as far as can be documented, final visit of Yeats to Bridges (now living near Oxford), on 19–21 June.[11] On that occasion Yeats learned that the anonymous author of *Charitessi, 1911* (1912) was in fact Bridges's daughter, Elizabeth. Perhaps with more exhilaration than critical judgment, Yeats wrote John Quinn on 24 June 1915 that 'I have just come from staying with Robert Bridges and the chief event there was the discovery that certain lofty, impassioned verses which have delighted me since their publication three years ago are his daughter's work. If she can add to their number she will be the most considerable poetess since Christina Rossetti.'[12]

Bridges invited Yeats to return to Chilswell in 1916, but

the Easter Rebellion and Yeats's visit to Normandy to join
Maud Gonne interfered. But when Yeats moved to Oxford at
the beginning of 1918, Bridges was one of his first visitors.[13]
And when he returned to Oxford in October 1919, Bridges
became a familiar caller. Joseph Hone notes that 'Bridges
seldom came into town without calling at 4 Broad Street. He
treated Yeats with affectionate nonchalance. "Don't think I
have come to see you," he would say when the door was
opened for him. "I have come for luncheon." '[14]

    After Yeats left Oxford permanently in March of 1922,
we find only a single exchange of letters about an unpaid visit
to Chilswell, and Bridges's letter a few months before his
death, sending Yeats a copy of *The Testament of Beauty* and
regretting that their friendship had almost dissolved through
lack of contact.

    When he learned of Bridges's death, Yeats sent his
widow a moving note of condolence. But a more public
tribute to .Bridges was forthcoming in *The Oxford Book of
Modern Verse* (1936). In that anthology Bridges, who seemed
to Yeats as he began his own career, 'a small Victorian poet
whose poetry, published in expensive hand-printed books,
one could find behind glass doors in the houses of wealthy
friends', is one of the handful of poets honored with a
separate section in the Introduction.[15] Yeats gives an honest
appraisal of the work of his old friend:

> Robert Bridges seemed for a time, through his influence
> on Laurence Binyon and others less known, the patron
> saint of the movement. His influence — practice, not
> theory, was never deadening; he gave to lyric poetry a
> new cadence, a distinction as deliberate as that of
> Whistler's painting, an impulse moulded and checked
> like that in certain poems of Landor, but different,
> more in the nerves, less in the blood, more birdlike, less
> human; words often commonplace made unforgettable
> by some trick of speeding and slowing,

> A glitter of pleasure
> And a dark tomb,

or by some trick of simplicity, not the impulsive simplicity of youth but that of age, much impulse examined and rejected:

> I heard a linnet courting
> His lady in the spring!
> His mates were idly sporting,
> Nor stayed to hear him sing
> His song of love. –
> I fear my speech distorting
> His tender love.

Every metaphor, every thought a commonplace, emptiness everywhere, the whole magnificent.[16]

Yeats included six poems by Bridges in the *Oxford Book* – all from *The Shorter Poems* (1894) and all but one among his established favorites for several decades. 'Weep not To-day' (Book V, No. 19) is the only lyric that Yeats had not previously commented on. 'The Storm is over' (Book IV, No. 23) and 'I heard a Linnet courting' (Book I, No. 5) he had quoted in his *Bookman* article in 1897; 'Muse and Poet' (Book II, No. 1) and 'Nightingales' (Book V, No. 12) had been sung to the psaltery by Florence Farr in 1901; and through reading 'On a Dead Child' (Book III, No. 4) Yeats had experienced 'an almost unendurable emotion' in November 1912.[17]

If Yeats's Bridges was a poet of the nineties, so too was Bridges's Yeats the author of the 1895 *Poems*. A glance at the respective libraries (see Appendices B and C) confirms that neither writer attempted to closely follow the other's career after their friendship had first been formed.

The relationship between Robert Bridges and W. B. Yeats, then, is perhaps more notable for its duration than for its intensity or its effect on their careers. Still, despite such obstacles as political differences and infrequent meetings it survived for over thirty years: it did so because it was founded on a deep and mutual respect for the art and craft of poetry.

NOTES TO THE INTRODUCTION

1. 'Books of the Week', *The Times* (London), 22 June 1894, p. 13.
2. 'The Poems of Mr. Bridges: A Brief and General Consideration', *The Century Guild Hobby Horse*, 6 (October 1891), pp. 148–60. The essay was used as the preface to *The Growth of Love* (Portland, Maine: T. B. Mosher, 1894), doubtless a pirated edition.
3. 'The Poetry of Robert Bridges,' *The Fortnightly Review*, 62 (July 1894), pp. 44–60. The essay was reprinted with the addition of a paragraph on *Nero: Part 2* in Dowden's *New Studies in Literature* (London: K. Paul, Trench, Trübner, 1895).
4. *A Book of Irish Verse*, selected from modern writers with an introduction and notes by W. B. Yeats (London: Methuen, 1895), p. 252. The Bridges poem (Book III, No. 19, of the *Shorter Poems*) is a translation from the French of Théophile Gautier, which is itself a translation of a poem by Thomas Moore. Yeats quotes all three versions to illustrate 'the gradual disappearance' of 'the vague rhythms and loose phrases' of Moore's poem.
5. Lady Gregory, *Our Irish Theatre: A Chapter of Autobiography*, The Coole Edition of Lady Gregory's Writings, IV (Gerrards Cross: Colin Smythe, 1972), 18. Lady Gregory misdates this conversation 1898; the correct date is supplied when the passage is quoted on p. 144.
6. 'Mr. Arthur Symons' New Book,' *The Bookman* (April 1897), in *Uncollected Prose by W. B. Yeats*, II, ed. John

P. Frayne and Colton Johnson (London: Macmillan, 1975), 40. Yeats reworked this passage into 'The Autumn of the Flesh,' published in the *Dublin Daily Express* for 3 December 1898 and included in *Literary Ideals in Ireland* (London: T. Fisher Unwin, 1899); it was retitled 'The Autumn of the Body' for *Ideas of Good and Evil* (London: A. H. Bullen, 1903). In the revised version Yeats calls Bridges 'a more considerable poet' than Lang, Gosse, or Dobson, and explains that he 'elaborated a rhythm too delicate for any but an almost bodiless emotion, and repeated over and over the most ancient notes of poetry, and none but these' (*Ideas of Good and Evil*, p. 299). The passage stands unchanged in the later reprintings of 'The Autumn of the Body', as in *Essays and Introductions* (London: Macmillan, 1961), p. 191.

7. Despite this disclaimer, Yeats still planned to have *The Return of Ulysses* produced by the 'Masquers Society' in 1903. In an unpublished letter to Gilbert Murray on 17 March 1903 (Bodleian Library), Yeats explained that the group had 'drawn up a list of plays for possible production – among these are Marlowe's Faustus, your translation of Hippolytus, a translation of Oedipus Tyrannus, a play of Congreve, a contemporary work of Robert Bridges (his "Return of Ulysses") and myself'. The Society collapsed before any plays were produced.

8. Although I doubt that Yeats ever made a conscious choice between Yattendon and Coole Park, it is interesting to observe George W. Russell (AE) writing to Lady Gregory in October 1897 that 'I suppose Willie Yeats is still in the West. I hope so, and may the Gods guard him there from the snares of Bridges who teaches him the false things in art . . . .' Quoted in *Uncollected Prose*, II, 26, from the typescript of Lady Gregory's Memoirs in the Berg Collection, New York Public Library.

9. *Men and Memories: Recollections of William Rothen-*

stein, 1878–1900 (London: Faber and Faber, 1931), p. 329.

10. For more details than are provided herein on Bridges's ultimately successful campaign, see *Imperfect Encounter: Letters of William Rothenstein and Rabindranath Tagore, 1911–1941*, ed. Mary M. Lago (Cambridge: Harvard University Press, 1972), esp. pp. 177–202.

11. Yeats wrote Lady Gregory that 'I spent Saturday to Monday at Oxford and with Robert Bridges, and had a very pleasant talkative visit. Bridges is a delightful person, both to look at and to listen to.' *Seventy Years: Being the Autobiography of Lady Gregory*, ed. Colin Smythe, The Coole Edition of Lady Gregory's Writings, XIII (Gerrards Cross: Colin Smythe, 1974), 486.

12. *The Letters of W. B. Yeats*, ed. Allan Wade (London: Rupert Hart-Davis, 1954), p. 596. Although Elizabeth Bridges (later Daryush) continued to publish her poems, Yeats seems to have quickly lost interest in her work.

13. Yeats wrote Lady Gregory on 12 January 1918 that 'Here I have so far only seen Walter Raleigh and Bridges' (*Letters*, p. 644).

14. Joseph Hone, *W. B. Yeats, 1865–1939*, 2nd ed. (London: Macmillan, 1962), p. 325.

15. *The Oxford Book of Modern Verse, 1892–1935*, chosen by W. B. Yeats (Oxford: Clarendon Press, 1936), p. v.

16. *Oxford Book*, pp. xvii–xviii. The first quotation is from *Achilles in Scyros* (London: Edward Bumpus, 1890), the second from one of the poems Yeats included in his selection. See also *Memoirs*, ed. Denis Donoghue (London: Macmillan, 1972), p. 225, for Yeats's entry in his 1909 journal that 'We were the second wave of the movement and had more passion because more confidence than the first — that of Bridges, Dobson, Lang.'

17. In his letter to Bridges on 25 April 1913, Yeats refers to the illness he described to H. J. C. Grierson on 14 November 1912 (*Letters*, p. 570).

The Correspondence, 1896 – 1930

Note

The following abbreviations are used in the headnotes to the letters:

BL British Library (Reference Division), Additional Manuscripts 55004. Cited by folio number.
IE *Imperfect Encounter: Letters of William Rothenstein and Rabindranath Tagore, 1911–1941*. Edited by Mary M. Lago. Cambridge: Harvard University Press, 1972. Cited by page number.

From ROBERT BRIDGES   Yattendon, Newbury
MS Bridges   1 June 1896

[John William Mackail (1859–1945) was a literary scholar and poet.]

Dear Sir

I have been reading your poems, which my friend Mr Mackail introduced me to. I write to tell you how much I admire a great deal of them, and what pleasure they gave me.

I know that I run the risk of being considered impertinent, but I had rather you shd think that than perhaps misinterpret my silence.

Hoping that you will excuse the liberty that I take in writing, & that you will write more and meet soon with the success which your work must ultimately reach,

I am, yours truly
ROBERT BRIDGES

From W. B. YEATS   Paris
MS Bridges   7 December [1896]

[Yeats's book was *The Secret Rose*, published in April 1897. Georg Brandes (1842–1927) was a Danish literary critic. Yeats refers to *Prometheus the FireGiver* (1883) and *Achilles in Scyros* (1890).]

Dear Sir:

When you wrote to me your kind letter about my verses, I postponed writing an answer out of sheer procrastination until I was ashamed to write without sending you the poor amends of a book of my verses or stories. A book of stories was on the point of coming out & I waited for it. It was however delayed & is now again delayed so that I must trust to no better help than my apologies. Your praise of my work gave me great pleasure as your work is to me the most convincing poetry done by any man among us just now. I said this to Brandes, the Norwegian, the other day, when he was praising all manner of noisy persons. Your work alone has the quietude of wisdom & I do most firmly believe that all art is dedicated to wisdom & not because it teaches anything but because it reveals divine substances. Your 'Achilles in Syros' and your 'Prometheus' have been to me a delight over a fair number of years now & only need a stage dedicated to wisdom, such as has been in many ages, to justify their form

[Unsigned]

From ROBERT BRIDGES   Yattendon, Newbury
MS Bridges   10 December 1896

[The postscript concerns the final line of 'Fergus [not Cuchulain] and the Druid', which read 'Lay hidden in the small slate-coloured bag!' in *The Countess Kathleen* (1892). In *Poems* (1895) Yeats changed 'bag!' to 'thing!'; in his copy of *Poems* Bridges noted his preference for 'bag!' Yeats was always uncertain about the line, retaining 'thing!' until 1908, reverting to 'bag!' from 1912 to 1924, trying 'thing!' again in 1925, using 'thing?' in 1927 and 1929, and finally settling on 'thing!' in 1933.]

Dear Sir
    Your letter is as great a surprise as it is a pleasure to me this morning – and as you date from a hotel I answer by return. When I wrote to you I purposely wrote such a letter as you could answer or not – for nothing is more tedious than admiration from people with whom one does not feel in sympathy – and had I said as much as I felt about your poetry you would have been constrained to thank me. As it was I was reconciling myself to the idea that you didn't care whether I liked your poetry or not. As a matter of fact I can read very little poetry so called – and your book is a great

exception. It has given me a great deal of delight, and I find magnificent things and very beautiful things in it. And it is most pleasant to me to hear that you have cared for my verse: and will therefore welcome my admiration for your work.

I hope when spring comes that you will consent to pay us a visit here. The country is pretty enough, tho' as you date your preface from Sligo I must not boast — still I feel safe from comparison because all is so different here.

I wonder what you are doing in Paris, and whether French farce delights you. I do not like Paris in the winter, but they have become more musical than they were when I used to be there.

I ought to say that your letter to me is unsigned — from which I hope I may conclude that you are in the middle of some piece of work which has got hold of you — I can not make a mistake however in recognising in it the answer to the only letter which I have written in the required sense.

Thank you very much for promising to send me your forthcoming book. I shd greedily buy anything of yours on the strength of the poems.

> Believe me
> Yours sincerely,
> ROBERT BRIDGES

I should like to write you some day about your poems, or better talk with you. — I think you have hit off one form (and really a new one as you do it) pe. fectly — in Cuchulin and the bag of dreams. By the way let *bag* stand in last line — why did you alter it? But I liked most of your alterations — I saw the 2 editions.

From W. B. YEATS   Paris
MS Bridges   10 January [1897]

[The 'dramatic poem' was *The Shadowy Waters*, which Yeats

was unsuccessfully trying to complete for publication by
Leonard Smithers (1861–1907). The novel was *The Speckled
Bird*, which Yeats eventually abandoned a few years after the
turn of the century.]

Dear Sir:
    A great many thanks for your letter. It was curious my
leaving mine unsigned. Your surmise, however, was right; I
was indeed & indeed am sunk in work, about which I am very
much in earnest. When I wrote I was more or less desperate
about a dramatic poem which refused to go faster than, my
average of some eight or nine lines a day, despite material
necessities that it should, & am still in a tempered
desperation. I am trying for a more remote wisdom, or peace
for they are much the same, & find it hard not to loose grip
on the necessary harvest of mere exterior beauty, in seeking
for this visionary harvest. I am doing my best work or my
worst & do not well know which. A thousand thanks for
your invitation to pay you a visit in the Spring. It will be a
great pleasure to do so. You are fortunate in being able to
live in the country where our mood[s] have a proper living
ritual to honour them. My work continually brings me to
cities. You wonder why I am in Paris & I can allege no better
reason than a novel, which I have undertaken to write, and
which brings its central personage from the Arran Islands to
Paris. I too would much like to discuss with you questions of
rhythm, for though I work very hard at my rhythm I have
but little science on the matter and as a result probably
offend often. Without a consistent science it is difficult to
distinguish between license and freedom. You are probably
write about the word 'bag' I changed it because of the
urgency of some one or other who thought the word ugly for
a close.

                              Yours ever
                              W B YEATS

I return to London next week & will be at 18 Woburn
Buildings Euston Road.

From ROBERT BRIDGES   Yattendon, Newbury
MS Bridges   8 March 1897

Dear Sir

Now that the weather seems to promise better I am writing to renew my invitation.

If a Saturday till Monday visit suits your work, that is convenient to us – but there is no objection to any other day.

The trains from London are
   Paddington   1.55 or 5.15
   arr *Newbury* where you change
         3.48 – 7.3
   and at Hampstead Norris (our station)
        4.11 7.31
If the 2nd trains happens to be late it is sometimes inconvenient for dinner arrangements.

I would meet you at Hampstead Norris by any train that you fix on.

We have only one spare bedroom in the house, so that unless we make a fixture some time beforehand I cannot promise to be able to put you up exactly under my roof, but I have another roof, at the end of my garden, where my friends often stay, a sort of dépendance, and I do not think that you would object to it, tho' I shd not like to ask you here without the warning, lest you shd think your reception discourteous.

I very much hope that you will come. You will be received in the name of a poet, & find others here besides myself who are friends of your work.

        believe me
        yours very truly
        R. BRIDGES

In case you shd choose a Sunday you may like to know that *Sunday clothes* are not particularly useful here, but evening clothes are sometimes convenient.

From W. B. YEATS   London
MS Bridges   16 March [1897]

[Yeats's article was 'Mr. Robert Bridges' (*Bookman*, June 1897). He may refer to either *Nero: Part I* (1885) or *Nero: Part 2* (1894). Bridges's edition of the *Poems* of Gerard Manley Hopkins (1844–89) was published in 1918. Yeats knew Hopkins only slightly but was well acquainted with Edward Dowden (1843–1913), Professor of English in Trinity College, Dublin.]

Dear Mr. Bridges:
    I have just got back from Ireland & found your letter waiting for me. A very great many thanks. May I come down on next Saturday week? I do not say next Saturday because I am just renewing my recollection of your plays, as a prelude to an article, which the Bookman asked me to do some time ago, but which has got postponed through my dislike of reading in the British Museum. I have now however got the books I wanted & will be through in about a week & will be able to talk of them. Your lyrics & one or two of the plays are too vivid to me to need a new memory; but some I read long ago; & Nero I am reading for the first time. My first reading of your work was in a book lent me by Prof Dowden a great many years ago. 'Prometheus the Firebringer' it was. I remember talking about it with your friend Father Hopkins, and discussing your metrical theories. I have been on an absurd crusade among absurd people & it will be a pleasure of the best to talk of poetry in the country. The roof at the garden end sounds charming.

                                        Yours sincerely
                                        W B YEATS

From ROBERT BRIDGES   Yattendon, Newbury
MS Bridges   17 March 1897

[The 'Books of the Week' column of *The Times* for 22 June 1894 devoted a paragraph to *Nero: Part 2*, concluding that it was 'essentially worth reading'.]

Dear Mr Yeats

I am very sorry indeed that you are engaged in such a dull task – and I am afraid that you may not be in a particularly good humour with me when you come – But let me reassure you on one point, i.e. that you need not be afraid of hurting my feelings, and are, as far as I am concerned, at full liberty to say anything that you wish. I lack that distinctive mark of the poet, the touchiness, which resents criticism. Honestly I am indifferent to these things: (and I don't mind if anyone shd say that I am vain of being proud –) – But you wd please me very much if you wd in your review say two things (1) whether the plays are *readable* – amusing, i.e. whether you want to put them down after you have begun them – because this is the main point. And (2) I should be glad of a plain statement that my plays are for sale at 2/6 each because the papers always make out that they cannot be bought or are privately printed, or out of print, or all three.

Nero pt. II, which completed my volume of 8 plays, was sent to 44 papers and reviews, and so far as I know it had *no* notice whatever except in the Times.

I shall look forward to your coming and hope to do away with any bad impression left by your surfeiting on my old work. Unfortunately the weather has gone back again – but I hope it will mend before end of next week. We have had, as far as the weather goes, a most wretched year.

Send me a line to say which train you come by – our station is Hampstead Norris – change at Newbury – from Paddington –

Yours very truly
R BRIDGES

From W. B. YEATS   London
MS Bridges   24 March [1897]

[Both *The Christian Captives* and *The Return of Ulysses* were published in 1890; Yeats's *Bookman* article concentrates on the latter.]

Dear Mr. Bridges:
    I will [come] by the 1.55 train from Paddington on Saturday next.
    I have now read all the plays except 'The Christian Captives' which I shall probably read before Saturday unless an unfortunate ballad of my own which has got to get done stop me. The Second Part of 'Nero,' & my old favourite 'Achilles in Scyros' & 'The Return of Ulysses' delight me most I think. I read the end of the Ulysses with the utmost excitement. You have held a clear mirror to the magnificent rush of the greatest of all poetry, the end of the Odyssey. It would be a fine thing on the stage & should get there in time.
                                    Yours ever
                                    W B YEATS

From ROBERT BRIDGES   Yattendon, Newbury
MS Bridges   30 March 1897

[Bridges refers to the lyric in 'The Rose of Shadow' in *The Secret Rose*. 'Rosa Alchemica' of the same collection ends with the apparent death of Michael Robartes. Bridges had married Mary Monica Waterhouse (1863–1949) in 1882.]

My dear Yeats
    We enjoyed your visit very much and I hope that you will think of Yattendon as a place where you might some day run down for a weeks country air and retirement in the summer.
    You left your dress shoes behind you. I sent them off

by parcel post today. I hope that they have reached you safely.

I have read most of the book and come to a great deal that I like very much, but it is so unlike anything that I know that I have not formed my judgement of it and shall not till I have reread it all carefully. I do not know whether you wd care to have it criticized. This is of course merely a practical question, as to whether you imagine I might chance to say something which wd be of use to you. If you wish for criticism you will let me know.

Today has been lovely. I wish Sunday had been like it. We took the children out into the woods, and gathered fircones. You did not see any of our woods, or rather forests: which I now much regret as they are our chief attraction.

By the way I liked some of the lyrics in the Secret Rose, especially "O what to me the little room" – I hope that you will take care of your body and that the saints or goddesses will preserve you from too much of the Rosa Alchemica. I am glad that Michael Robartes is dead.

My wife joins in kindest regards.

> believe me
> yours very sincerely
> R BRIDGES

From W. B. YEATS   Sligo
MS Bridges   [6 June 1897]

[Yeats was staying with George Pollexfen (1839–1910). *The Celtic Twilight* had been published in 1893 by A. H. Bullen (1857–1920).]

My dear Mr Bridges:

You will have enough knowledge of my delays in answering letters to understand that when I did not write in answer to your last letter & ask you to tell me what you thought of 'The Secret Rose', it was from no lack of desire for your opinion but shere procrastination as usual. I am now in Sligo with an uncle who reduces my habits into order as a mangle does clothes. He is the genius of regularity & the result is that when ever I get here I begin to think of my sins & to answer letters steadily. Did you get 'The Celtic Twilight' which I asked Bullen to send you? Could you without taking too much trouble tell me what you think of it & of 'The Secret Rose[']? If you tell me the parts you like best & the parts you like worst, it will not be much trouble, & will be useful to me.

My article on your work is in the Bookman this month & I have asked them to send you a copy: you must not judge it as you would judge an essay meant to be permanent. It is merely conscientious journalism like all my criticism so far, & done more quickly than I would like. One has to give something of one's self to the devil that one may live. I have given my criticism.

Yours ever

W B YEATS

From ROBERT BRIDGES   Yattendon, Newbury
MS Bridges   9 June 1897

[Rosses Point is near Sligo.]

My dear Yeats
    I am very glad to hear from you, and a letter from you will always be a surprise. I have been away from home, and am now settled in for the summer, hoping that it will bring among its delights a visit from you. Please come and see us again as soon as you can, and take up your abode here for awhile.
    I am going today to Oxford for two days – and . . . No that is quite wrong. I am just starting for Newbury – and shall be back this evening – so I shall be able to write to you tomorrow or next day concerning the 'Celtic Twilight.' I did

not write before about it, not knowing where you were nor whether you wished to have anything said about it. I shall be glad to tell you just what I think both on the chance of something being useful and also to improve our acquaintance, which I pray may grow – I admire most your gifts of poetry and humour and hope that you will cultivate them at the cost of everything else. Poetry does not get stronger in a man as he gets older – whereas the humour of him does[.] There fore write poetry. Thanks for telling them to send me the Bookman. You do me great honour in writing of my works. I will take it as you desire. Handel said of his routine stuff 'A gentlemen must do something to live.' I am afraid you must give your uncle a good deal of trouble[.] You can point out to him you know a man who has answered a letter by return of post – I will send you a letter soon on the Secret Rose & the Twilight. If I delay a day or so it will be spent in fresh study of the volumes.

Yours sincerely
R BRIDGES

How I should like a day or two at Rosses Point!!

From ROBERT BRIDGES   Yattendon, Newbury
[?]   15 June 1897

[The location of the holograph of this letter is unknown. The text below combines the long excerpt in Joseph Hone's *W. B. Yeats, 1865–1939* (London: Macmillan, 1943), pp. 135–36, with a rather faulty transcription in the collection of Senator Michael B. Yeats. Each version has been silently corrected; ellipses are used where no text survives.

Laurence Binyon (1869–1943) was a poet and a mutual friend of Bridges and Yeats. Bridges quotes from 'Regina, Regina Pigmeorum, Veni' in *The Celtic Twilight*; he refers to 'Rosa Alchemica', the last story in *The Secret Rose*, and to 'The Crucifixion of the Outcast'. In his *Bookman* article,

Yeats had quoted the final two stanzas of No. 23 of Book IV of *The Shorter Poems*. The anonymous reviewer of the same collection in *The Athenaeum* for 21 February 1891 had quoted all of the poem and commented: 'This sort of metre, without cadence recognizable to the English ear – though it may, by the laws of scanning, satisfy some accentual prosody intended by Mr. Bridges – and without flow, is gratuitously unnatural, and makes very harsh verse.' Most of Bridges's work in *The Yattendon Hymnal* (1895–99) consisted of translation or adaptation.]

My dear Yeats

I was at Oxford on Friday and Saturday and on Sunday had two visitors here, one was Binyon, the other a man I have never met before who was quite enthusiastic about your work especially the two volumes of tales. I had read the two books again with the intention of fulfilling my promise of writing to you about them, so I discussed with him the judgment that I had arrived at and found that he quite agreed with me and this I confess made me hesitate less in telling you the one criticism I have to make without further consideration.

I think that the stories are artistically the worse for the apparent insistence on the part of the writer to have them taken otherwise (*i.e.* more seriously) than he suspects the reader would naturally take them.

Of course I know that it is your intention that they should be so taken. Only I do not think that the intention should appear. The manner of presentation should be sufficient and I do not see you need distrust the power of your presentation.

This is rather a subtle matter, because in looking again at the stories I don't quite see where I get my impression of this "insistence" from. I fancy it lies chiefly in your sometimes just overstepping the mark, *e.g.* in "Regina Pigmeorum" the sentence "I asked the young girl etc." will not fail to make readers wonder at the personality of the

An 1897 drawing of Robert Bridges by William Rothenstein.
From *English Portraits* (1898)

An early photograph of Robert Bridges. From *The Bookman* (London), December 1898

A 1912 photograph of Robert Bridges, the frontispiece to *Poetical Works* (1912)

Bridges as Poet Laureate. From the *Illustrated London News,* 26 July 1913

November 1896 portrait of W. B. Yeats by John Butler Yeats. First published in the *Literary Year-Book 1897*

An early photograph of W. B. Yeats. From *The Outlook* (New York), 2 January 1904

An 1898 lithograph of W. B. Yeats by William Rothenstein.
Reproduced in *Liber Juniorum* (1899)

A 1908 photograph of W. B. Yeats. From D. J. Gordon, *W. B. Yeats, Images of a Poet* (1961)

writer – I should like to talk this over with you some day when we can refer to places in the stories. I should not have liked to offer the objection if my feeling about it had not been very strong, and if I had not found another admirer with exactly the same impression.

Reading the stories again made me admire the workmanship more than ever. The gentleman in question said that he thought the prose style better than any that he knew and I am inclined to agree with him. – It is extremely beautiful.

Omitting the last story of the Secret Rose I don't know that I have anything to mention that seemed to me below level. Some of the stories of course are more telling and interesting than others – I do not however fall in comfortably with the humour of crucifying the beggar. The accounts of the [. . .] are splendid – and the humour all thro' is of the best.

I expect that while we agree absolutely about the necessity for [. . .] we do not take quite the same view of the value of phenomena in themselves, but I can't write about this.

When I received "The Secret Rose" I marked a number of places where I thought a slight alteration of words would improve the flow, or where it seemed to me you had made a slip. I should like to go over these with you some day in view of a new edition. It seems to me that these stories are an excellent proof that English "short stories" may be written in as good style as the best French ones. I hope you will do more short stories of Irish life – I am not in the least overestimating my admiration of your style. I am *very grateful* to you for presenting me with these two volumes – and I shall try and profit by them. The writing is (I'd have said) too good for success in journalism – Is it not so? No one has ever told me of it – Perhaps the somewhat bizarre character of the subjects puts people off the mark.

Please come and see us again before long and be assured meanwhile of my blessing and high esteem.

Yours very sincerely
R. BRIDGES

P.S. Thanks for the "Bookman" I was forgetting about it. I was pleased that you posted as an example of good rhythm the same lines that the Athenaeum quoted us as a sample of bad rhythm. This is as it should be. Also you amused my wife much by numbering "The Yattendon Hymnal" among my original works – Many thanks for the trouble which you took with my things reading them etc.

From ROBERT BRIDGES   Yattendon, Newbury
MS Bridges   30 June 1899

[Yeats's 'Mr. Moore, Mr. Archer and the Literary Theatre' (*The Daily Chronicle*, 30 January 1899) took issue with some remarks by the drama critic William Archer (1856–1924). In 'The Theatre', printed in *The Dome* for April 1899 and included in the first issue of *Beltaine* in May 1899, Yeats had remarked that 'Mr. Bridges' *Return of Ulysses*, one of the most beautiful and, as I think, dramatic of modern plays, might have some success in the Arran Islands, if the Gaelic League would translate it into Gaelic, but I am quite certain that it would have no success in the Strand'. *The Feast of Bacchus* was published in 1889, *The Wind Among the Reeds* in April 1899. Yeats had in fact written to Bridges twice in 1897 from 18 Woburn Buildings. The second volume of Bridges's *Poetical Works* was published on 1 November 1899. Bridges refers to the theological controversies surrounding the first production of *The Countess Cathleen* on 8 May 1899.]

My dear Yeats

I was very glad to get a line from you, and to hear something of your theatre. I take a great interest in it, but don't of course hear much down here. I was fortunate one day, being on the railway, & buying a "Chronicle" to hit off your letter on the Drama, aimed at some conventional critic. I liked it extremely, and it seemed unanswerable. I hope that your Dublin plays will be a yearly thing, and that they will pay their expences. As for London, it is hopeless at present – it is all scenery and low 'fun', with some fashionable rant. I expect it was never much better, but the conventions just now are the deadliest dreariness. Thanks for attending to "Ulysses" – I don't expect (or really wish) to see a play of mine on the stage, but I feel confident that when the "Feast of Bacchus" gets there, it will stay. Still that is not much in your line.

A thousand thanks for "The Wind among the Reeds." I shall value extremely a copy with your inscription, but you do me wrong in imagining that I am not among your buyers. I got the book as soon as it came out. How then did I not write to congratulate you and thank you for it? I don't know where to write to you, and that uncertainty always prevents me from writing a letter. It's like talking to a man who may not be in the room. If you will send me an address whence letters are always forwarded to you I will trouble you from time to time with my praises & salutations. It happens that you have never written to me twice from the same place. Now it is Galway.

This is a good place except in winter. Spring and autumn are not bad, and I hope that you may come in autumn. We are free of all hat and coat conventions, and you wd find it quiet here, and easy to work: and could stay on as you liked.

The new poems delighted me. There are things I don't understand – but that is all the better. I am very glad that you have got so much recognition, it is really very lucky, tho' I don't suppose you can have a very large sale. Still enough to pay a little I expect. To publish at a loss is most depressing.

I have a new volume of "Collected Works" (a sad sign of

age) coming out in October. 1/3 of the book will be more or less new, & hoping there may be some among the new poems that you will like I will send you a copy if I know where to send it.

Accept, as the French say, the tribute of my lofty and unimpaired esteem

Yours sincerely
ROBERT BRIDGES

I am glad the Papists went for you! They are very cheeky just now.

From ROBERT BRIDGES   Yattendon, Newbury
MS Bridges   18 June 1901

['Wandering and milky smoke' is a quotation from 'The Wanderings of Oisin', which Bridges was reading in the 1895 *Poems*. Elkin Mathews (1851–1921) was the publisher of *The Wind Among the Reeds*.]

My dear Yeats
    I am sorry never to have a chance of meeting you. Binyon was here the other day and brought some tidings. I hope that you and the Muse are getting on well. Is it *possible* that you will honour us by another visit this summer? – some Sunday when you have nothing better to do? I am writing today because by some accident I took up your 'Poems' yesterday, and I have been reading at them ever since, with the same admiration and delight, but all fresh because of my bad memory – the best gift that I have. – I forget what time of year it was when you were here. I rather think it may have been about this time – it is not bad – a little over green – I think you would like the quiet if you cd stay long enough to taste it. Do you think you cd come some Saturday till Monday? There is a very first class train from Paddington to Pangbourne of an evening. It leaves Padding-

ton at 6.10 and its wandering and milky smoke does not stop at Reading. You must get into the right carriage which is slipped after Reading for the little stations. We wd send to Pangbourne to meet you. I suppose that Elkin Mathews will send this on to you. I don't know whether your old address is of any use. Please come if you can.

Yours sincerely
ROBT BRIDGES

From ROBERT BRIDGES   Yattendon, Newbury
MS Bridges   8 July 1901

[Elizabeth Waterhouse (1834–1918) was gathering the material for her *A Little Book of Life and Death*, published in June 1902; the book was part of the 'Little Library' of the firm founded by Sir Algernon Methuen Marshall (1856–1924). Waterhouse included 'The Lake Isle of Innisfree' and 'The Sorrow of Love' (which begins 'The quarrel of the sparrows in the eaves').]

My dear Yeats

My mother in law Mrs. Waterhouse is making a book for one of Methuen's series & has asked me to ask you if she may insert in it the following poems of yours

    "The Isle of Innisfree
    The sorrow of love
or   "the quarrel of the sparrows"
I know nothing of the book so please regard the request as from her and not from me.

I wish you wd come and see us some day. We shall after this week be at home till end of summer.

Anyhow just send me a line about this matter.

Yours ever
R BRIDGES

From W. B. YEATS   Coole Park
MS Bridges   20 July [1901]

[Yeats's poem was 'Baile and Aillinn' (*The Monthly Review*, July 1902). *Cuchulain of Muirthemne* by Lady Gregory (1852–1932) was published in April 1902. Yeats was working with the musician Arnold Dolmetsch (1858–1940) and the actress Florence Farr (1860–1917) in perfecting the art of 'Speaking to the Psaltery'. 'The Nightingales' was published in *Shorter Poems, Book V* (1893). 'Muse and Poet' is Yeats's title for the lyric 'Will love again awake' in *Poems* (1879); this became the first poem of Book II of the *Shorter Poems* (1890). Yeats included both poems in *The Oxford Book of Modern Verse* (1936).]

My dear Mr. Bridges:
      Certainly Mrs. Waterhouse may include 'The Lake Isle of Innisfree' and 'The Sorrow of Love' in her book. I confess I grow not a little jealous of the 'Lake Isle' which has put the noses of all my other children out of joint; & I am not very proud of 'The Sorrow of Love' – I wonder does she know my book 'The Wind among the Reeds' – but as she will.
      I shall be away all summer for I shall not leave Ireland until after the performances by 'The Irish Literary Theatre' which begin on Oct 21. I shall hardly be back until early November. Might I not run down to you for a winter day or two. The country is always beautiful whatever the season.
      I take up your letter again & notice to my distress that it is dated June 18 but the reason of the delay is that I have been moving about & so have only just opened the box of books & letters, which my housekeeper in London sent on to me here.
      I am writing a half lyrical half narrative poem on two old Irish lovers, Baile, Honey Mouth & one Alyinn – to write the names as they are spoken. I then go on to other stories of the same epoch. I have in fact begun what I have always meant to be the chief work of my life – The giving life not to

a single story but to a whole world of little stories, some not indeed very little, to a romantic region, a sport [sort] of enchanted wood. The old Irish poets wove life into life thereby giving to the wildest & strangest romance, the solidity & vitality [of] the *Comedie Humaine*, & all this romance was knitted into the scenery of the country. 'Here at this very spot the faery woman gave so & so the cup of magic meed. Not there by the hillock but here by the Rock' & so on. This work has not been possible to me hitherto, partly because my verse was not plastic enough & partly for lack of a good translations. But now my friend Lady Gregory has made the most lovely translation putting the old prose & verse not into the pedantic 'hedge school master' style of her predecessors, but into a musical caressing English, which never goes very far from the idioms of the country people she knows so well. Her book, which she is about two thirds through, will I think take its place between the *Morte D'Arthur* & The *Mabinogion*.

I have a notion of getting one of these stories, in which there are dialogues in verse spoken by a reciter who will chant the dialogues to a psaltry. Dolmetsch has interested himself in the chanting – about which you ask me – and has made a psaltry for Miss Farr. It has 12 strings, one for each note in her voice. She will speak to it, speaking an octave lower than she sings. In our experiments in London we found your verse the most suited of all verse to this method. She recites, your 'Nightingales' your 'Muse & poet' and a third poem of yours whose name I forget. You should hear her but had better wait until she has got used to the Psaltry & has perfected the method with Dolmetsch a little more. We found that the moment a poem was chanted one saw it in a quite new light – so much verse that read well spoke very ill. Miss Farr has found your verse & mine [&] a little modern lyric verse to be vocal, but that when one gets back a few generations lyric verse ceases to be vocal until it gets vocal as song not as speach is, as one approaches the Elizabethans. We had great difficulty even with Keats & though we got a passage which is splendidly vocal we had to transpose a line because of a construction, which could only be clear to the eye which can see several words at once.

I shall be altogether content if we can perfect this art for I have never felt that reading was better than an error, a part of the fall into the flesh, a mouthful of the apple.

Yours sinly
W B YEATS

From ROBERT BRIDGES   Yattendon, Newbury
MS Bridges   24 July 1901

[The novelist Thomas Anstey Guthrie (1856–1934) used the pen-name 'Anstie'. Bridges's book was the new edition of *Milton's Prosody*, published in December 1901).]

My dear Yeats
    Thank you for your permission to Mrs Waterhouse, which I will transmit to her. I do not warrant her book, in fact her taste is not as mine in anything. But these things have to be left to go as they will – and it is after all some sort of consolation that there shd be people who 'appreciate' that part of one's work which one does not care for oneself. I have always said that if I had published what I had burned & burned what I had published I shd have been a popular poet. Quite a echo of the age & a man of the day.
    I am sorry that we have missed you but you must come in the winter and make up – don't forget. And the dusk and the fireside will be a better atmosphere for you to tell the children some of your Irish legends.
    I am much interested in all that you say about your work – and very much pleased that you are able to carry out your scheme. Your style in lyric & narrative is alike most charming* to me and I shd think that a combination of the two should show you at your best. The trouble of lyric verse is, I fancy, that it needs a mood which is fitful and really

impossible to sustain – it is of its nature to exhaust itself and break off – whereas the narrative, tho' it may really be as full of imagination, or seem to be, when once started has a tendency to run on of itself. So that with this to fall back on you need never be idle.

I agree about the recitation, I think. It is a very difficult matter. Setting *song* aside – which has several degrees – the mere reading of poetry, if well read, is full of melodious devices, which it is the art of a good reader to conceal, so that he gets his effects without calling attention to them. The word recitation – and the presence of an instrument – makes open confession of his art, and without becoming a singer he ceases to be a reader. The hearer has his attention called to the method itself – and as I have never had any experience of good chanting or recitation I do not know how I shd like it. There was a kind of recitation fashionable some years ago in London drawing rooms – satirized by Anstie – and it even crept into the churches. I have heard the Old Testament 'recited' in Westminister Abbey. This used to draw tears from me – tears of laughter. I shook as at a French farce. This is the only sort that I ever heard. I can't really imagine a recitation which I shd myself like as well as good reading (in which the same art wd be disguised) but I think that there must be such a thing – and I hope you and the lady will discover it.

I will send you a book with some interesting poetic notes in it before the autumn.

Yours ever
R BRIDGES

*In the right sense of the word

From ROBERT BRIDGES   Chilswell, near Oxford
MS Bridges   15 November 1907

[Elizabeth Waterhouse was now preparing *Companions of the Way: Being Selections for Morning and Evening Reading,* published in October 1908; she included eight selections from Yeats's poems and plays. Bridges had moved to Chilswell earlier in 1907.]

My dear Poet
      I have not heard that you have got married since I saw you last, therefore you must rely on your dramatic imagination to tell you what you wd do if your mother-in-law were an anthologist and she were to ask you to make use of the slight friendship between us (which you have so selfishly neglected) to persuade me to allow her to print some of my poems in her anthology. It is as you may have guessed Mrs Waterhouse of Yattendon who insists on approaching you in this roundabout way, and I enclose her request. She anthologises for Methuen who gives her a good price for her work and agrees to pay fees for copyright poems up to a certain limit. The anthology is a religious "day-book." I have now done my duty, and I leave her in your hands. If you look thro' the list (which I have not done) you will be able to see whether you can fix any price for Methuen to pay. I do not wish that out of kindness to me you shd do anything unusual. I have a great abhorrence of these anthologists, tho' I now and then get something out of them. But I believe that the multiplication of their poetry books does really hinder the sale of poems.
      I have built a home up here. Everything is new. — It was a barren waste. If ever you shd feel at all kindly disposed to me we shd be glad to see you, but Summer is better than Winter. It is a pleasant place, very near Oxford, on a hill, solitary.

Yours very sincerely
ROBERT BRIDGES

You can reply to me or to Mrs W Yattendon Court.

From ROBERT BRIDGES   Chilswell, near Oxford
MS Bridges   20 April 1913

[Rabindranath Tagore's *Gitanjali* was published in a limited
edition for the India Society late in 1912. In the introduction
Yeats had explained that 'Four-fifths of our energy is spent
in the quarrel with bad taste, whether in our own minds or in
the minds of others.' The literary scholar William John
Courthope (1842–1917) and the writer Edmund Gosse
(1849–1928) were, like Yeats and Bridges, members of the
Academic Committee of the Royal Society of Literature. The
meeting probably concerned the award of the Polignac Prize.
Walter Raleigh (1861–1922) was Professor of English Literature at Oxford.]

My dear Yeats
    Binyon brought us Tagore's poems with your lovely
preface. What a delight it was! O most blessed one! there is
no one but you who could write so. He told me that it was
coming out in a cheap edition – and he promised to give you
a message from me, the practical part of which was that I
want you to alter one word in your masterpiece. It is the
expression "four fifths" or "five sixths", or something of
that fractional quality. He did not see the point, but you will.
    It led me to wondering what fractions could be
admitted into that consummate style. A half is of course all
right; and perhaps 2/3, because 3 is the mystic subdivision of
all things, and 2/3 might be called "two parts". But after that
one falls into conversational meaninglessness.
    Last time I had the happiness of seeing you, you were
sitting in Committee with Messrs Courthope, Gosse and
others, and were so much interested that I could not speak
with you!
    Will you never come & see us again? You are not always
attended, I take it, by your company of players. Term begins
today, and there are sympathetic souls who wd be rejoiced to
meet you: above all Walter Raleigh – and my house is retired

on a hill, & has a large room, library and music room, where you cd do what you liked. Really you wd not do badly – I, though I am getting very old, am still alive. I can't however think of anything to attract you, unless honest flattery can draw. Anyhow it's better than London Committees with Gosse and Co.

Really I write this lest Binyon shd not have told you about that 4/5. It came to me as a discord. But if you don't feel it, there is a chance that I may be wrong: but I don't think so.

So come and see us this Spring before the hyacinths are over. The Spring is very beautiful in our woods. We are quite in the country, but can walk across fields & ferry to Oxford in 40 minutes.

Yours in poetic devotion
ROBERT BRIDGES

Don't feel obliged to write a letter. – a postcard, or 4/5 of a postcard wd tell me you will come.

From W. B. YEATS   London
MS Bridges   25 April [1913]

[The commercial edition of *Gitanjali* was published in March 1913. Yeats never eliminated the 'four-fifths'. Bridges's 'On A Dead Child' was first published in *Poems* (1880) and reprinted in Book III of *Shorter Poems* (1890). Yeats included it in the *Oxford Book of Modern Verse*.]

My dear Mr Bridges:

You are quite right about that fraction & if I should ever reprint the essay (the popular edition is out) I will change it. I am very grateful for your praise, no other man's could have the same worth for me. I had a short illness six months ago & the first sign of returning health was the excitement of finding that I could read poetry again & the poem that brought me this excitement was your poem on the dead child. In my weak state it produced an almost unendurable emotion.

I will write & invite myself to come & see you a little later. My players to whom I am always a little tied though I seldom now stage-manage or the like return from America next week, & for a week or two after that I shall be busy over financial details & so on. I thank you for asking me.

Yours always

W B YEATS

From ROBERT BRIDGES   Chilswell, near Oxford
MS Bridges   7 December [1913]

[Bridges is referring to the salutation of Yeats's last letter. The writer and critic Logan Pearsall Smith (1865–1945) was one of the founders with Bridges of the Society for Pure English. The original Prospectus was issued in October 1913. Although Yeats noted on this letter 'should write and join society', his name does not appear on the lists of S.P.E. members issued in 1948. Yeats, Ezra Pound (1885–1972), and others were organizing a tribute for the writer Wilfrid Scawen Blunt (1840–1922), well-known for his opposition to English imperialism. The festivities were eventually held at Blunt's estate in Sussex on 18 January 1914.]

My dear *Mr* Yeats

I hope you like the *Mr.* At any rate I am grateful to you for not calling me Dr.

I send you as you request another copy of the S.P.E. Proposals. Pearsall Smith tells me that people responded well so I hope we shall soon be proceeding to business.

As for your main matter. I really can have nothing to do with Restaurant dinners. You can't imagine how I dislike them & all their adjuncts. I admire Wilfrid Blunt's work, but he has unfortunately a very political or impolitical side, & I do not know enough about that to feel quite comfortable about what one might let oneself in for if one was to magnify him ostensibly. So pray excuse me.

I am sorry that you never managed to come and see us this year. Now that the weather makes so much mud between us & Oxford I can only look forward to next year. I do hope that you will come then – in the spring if possible.

Yours very sincerely
ROBT BRIDGES

From ROBERT BRIDGES   Chilswell, near Oxford
MS Bridges   3 May 1915

[The book Bridges was preparing for Charles James Longman (1852–1934) was *The Spirit of Man: An Anthology in English & French from the Philosophers and Poets made by the Poet Laureate in 1915* (1916). The 'Oriental man' was Hasan Shahid Suhrawardy, a student at Oxford.]

Private
My dear Yeats

Longman the Publisher who lost his son early in the war asked me to make him up a volume of consolatory poetry. I think that was his idea. I told him that I did not believe in the benefits of consolatory poems, but that if he liked I wd make a book that I thought people in distress would like to read. He came round to my notion of the book and putting it together has been a great distraction to me ever since last Xmas. It is nearly done now. It is a very serious performance and I think unlike anything that has been done before.

Of course I am writing to ask your permission to insert certain of your poems. It is really absolutely necessary that you shd consent – and I believe that if you saw my book you wd readily agree to my proposition. I can hardly give you a notion of it, but I can tell you a few points. French is admitted equally with English. All other languages are translated, and the authors who show most solid are Plato, Aristotle, Homer[,] Shelley[.] Other names are Spinoza[,] Augustine[,] Gregory the Great, Pascal, Descartes[,] Keats, Wordsworth, Milton, etc[.] Then Oriental poems are set alongside of the Greek and English, and the juxtaposition from Spinoza & Keats, Augustine & Shelley, you and Aristotle will show people what poetry means.

I find that very little modern poetry will stand up among these people, but you are an exception and your "Sad Shepherd" and "The Man who dreamed of Fairyland" come by their own. I want these, & "Innisfree" and two other short pieces.

Now for heaven's sake write and tell me that I may use them in this way. I am not going to buy much modern verse so I will tell Longman that he must pay your fees. Only be generous, and do not ask him a prohibitory price.

I am quite sure that the way in which I set your poems will do them a lot of good. For people do not recognize the extreme beauty & mastery of the Shepherd and the Fairyland man.

I hope you are well. I shall be very anxious for your answer.

Yours ever
R B

I have a very good Oriental man working his department with me. If you wish to know more about my book I will tell you anything I can – or will you not come here? You have promised us a visit. & now the bluebells are coming out in our wood. I have done almost all the translations myself –

From W. B. YEATS   London
MS Bridges   [9 May 1915]

[T. Fisher Unwin (1848–1935) had published many of Yeats's early poems. Henry More (1614–87) was one of the Cambridge Platonists.]

My dear Mr Bridges:

Of course. I am honoured that you should quote me and flattered. If Unwin asks too much — he has some fixed tarif which I forget — I will get him to abate his price, & the same with Bullen. If you like I will write to them first. I hope I have not left this too long unanswered. I have been moping because day after day I was reading Henry More & a lot of old witch trials to avoid doing a piece of very hard writing & was therefore in a state of wretchedness. I could not attend to anything but now that I have got to work again I have begun setting things in order.

I would very much like to go down to you but cannot till my players go back to Dublin — they are at the "little theatre" & shall be all May. Thank you for asking me.

Yours
W B YEATS

From ROBERT BRIDGES   Chilswell, near Oxford
MS Bridges   13 May [1915]

[Bridges refers to Sir Frederick Macmillan (1851–1936). Bridges was trying to obtain permission to revise one of the poems from *Gitanjali* for inclusion in *The Spirit of Man*. On 22 March 1915 Tagore wrote to Bridges, explaining that 'permission rests with my publishers, who, I am sure, will not refuse you'. He added that he was 'grateful for any help I get from such masters of word-music in English as you are. But as the Gitanjali poems have already become popular, any alteration in their rhythm is likely to be unwelcome to readers familiar with them' (BL 183). A day later Tagore wrote to Macmillan, suggesting that he refuse permission for both the use of the poem and the alterations (see BL 34). Tagore explained in a letter to the artist William Rothenstein (1872–1945) on 4 April 1915 that 'I cannot accept any help from Bridges excepting where the grammar is wrong or wrong words have been used' (IE 195).]

My dear Yeats

(do not call me Mr) I am very much obliged to you for your kindness about the poems and you *must* come here before the spring is over and see my book. I am sure that you will like my scheme, and wish to have a finger in it.

Today I am busier than usual, and shall be for some days longer. When I am free I will write you a letter about Tagore's publisher, who is giving me trouble. I want to insert *one* of his poems, & I can't get Macmillan to allow me to alter one or two words.

Yours ever
R BRIDGES

I have been away from home and am just returned. Hence my incommodities and delay.

From ROBERT BRIDGES   Chilswell, near Oxford
MS Bridges   6 June 1915

[Bridges's daughter was Elizabeth Bridges (1887–1977), who married A. A. Daryush (1899–   ) in 1923.]

My dear Poet.

I have it noted on your last letter that I wrote some thanks for it on May 13th. I did not write you a full letter then because you said you were so engaged with your actors. But now I hope that I may be able to persuade you to pay us a visit. You will find perfect quiet here and a bracing air – we are on the top of a hill, with a wood behind the house. Wife and one daughter at home. If you wd come for a few days at least we shd be so much delighted. Do please come, you need not bring any tidy clothes. I shd like nothing better. And then I cd tell you about my book. I am sure that it will please you. About my selection from your poems, you kindly said that you wd write to your publisher about it. I will let you know later exactly what I want: but I can't expect you to

favour my scheme without knowing more about it. In any case I shall make my publisher pay for your poems. I could not do my book without them. I was completely set at rest on this point by your kindness in trusting me. Now, what day will you come? I will meet you at G W R station if you will let me know the train. It is such an easy journey. At any rate you might afford me one night, leaving London by the 4.50 (or 55) p.m. & returning to town next midday or afternoon.
    Come!

Yours ever
R BRIDGES

If you *won't* come let me know if you are meetable in town, at Austrian Cafe some day —

From ROBERT BRIDGES   Chilswell, near Oxford
MS Bridges   14 June [1915]

[C. H. St. John Hornby (1867—1946) had printed Bridges's *Poems Written in the Year MCMXIII* (1914). The friend was Lionel Boulton Campbell Lockhart Muirhead (1845—1925), whom Bridges had known since their days at Eton together.]

My dear Yates
    We are delighted. Saty next to Monday will suit us very well. It happens that St. John Hornby (who prints) and his wife are coming for that week-end. Neither I nor my wife have ever met either of them, but he has lately printed a book for me, & knows a friend of mine very well. Hence the visit. I tell you in case there shd be any reason why you shd not wish to meet them — blood-feud or other scruple. Walter Raleigh is coming to dine on Sunday.
    We told the Hornby's to come by the train that leaves Paddington at 1.45 on Saty aftn. If that suits you you cd come up from Oxford by the same motor trip.
    It would be a convenience to let us know, as soon as

you cd tell us, what train you will come by. In any case we will send to meet the train.

Yours ever
R B

I want to show you my book. And I may get some hints from you.

From W. B. YEATS   London
MS Bridges   23 June [1915]

[*Cathay* was published earlier in 1915. Elizabeth Bridges's *Charitessi, 1911* was published anonymously in 1912. She acknowledged its authorship in her next volume, *Verses* (1916).]

Dear Mr. Bridges:
   I send you Ezra Pounds 'Cathay' his book of Chinese translations.
   I have just read once more all through your daughters book. It is certainly the best poetry done by any woman in our time.
   I thank you & Mrs. Bridges for a visit that has given me great pleasure.

Yours ev
W B YEATS

From W. B. YEATS   London
MS Bridges   30 June [1915]

[Yeats sent Bridges *The Green Helmet* (1912) and Lady Gregory's *Cuchulain of Muirthemne* (1902) and *Gods and Fighting Men* (1904).]

Dear Mr Bridges:

I send you a copy, a hateful American copy decorated in my despite, of "the Green Helmet" & also Lady Gregorys two books which you need not return. I think these two books of hers very beautiful 'Gods & fighting men' especially is full of fine Lyric passages. In the other book read especially the lamentation of Dierdre at the end of her story & the Emer lamentation at the end of the book.

I have been reading your daughters work to a number of people who admire it as much as I do. I have done some poems not yet published & I will try to let you have copies when I can get them typed.

Yours siny

W B YEATS

From ROBERT BRIDGES   Chilswell, near Oxford

MS Bridges   5 July [1915]

[*A Selection from the Poetry of W. B. Yeats* was published as a Tauchnitz Edition early in 1913. Bridges requests permission to include 'The Lover Tells of the Rose in His Heart', 'The Lake Isle of Innisfree', 'The Pity of Love', 'The Sad Shepherd', 'The Man Who Dreamed of Faeryland', 'Into the Twilight', 'The Ragged Wood', and 'He Wishes for the Cloths of Heaven'. On the letter Yeats has indicated that rights for the first five are held by T. Fisher Unwin, the last three by A. H. Bullen.]

My dear Yeats,

Thank you very much for the gift of the two books which came on Saturday. I value them greatly, and feel quite unworthy of the inscription in the poems. I did not know that you were in "Tauchnitz," and am interested to have a copy. Elizab" and I are searching for some more short passages to put in to the book where the prose is too thick, but I consider that the book is virtually done.

I looked thro' it last night to see what quotations I had from you, and I found 8 pieces.

1 All things uncomely.
2 I will arise and go.
3 A pity beyond all telling
4 Sad Shepherd
5 Man who dreamed of fairyland
6 Out worn heart (first stanza)
7 O hurry where by.
8 Had I the heavens' . .

I have made this list out in order that you may tell me, if you have the time, and can do it without trouble, to what publishers I shd apply for leave to use these things. Longman understands that he will have to pay for them.

Also I shd like to know what your feelings are about punctuation. That is whether the punctuation in your editions represents your view of what the rhythmical reading requires.

I want especially to know whether the punctuation of (7) "Ragged woods" is as you wish it. In my opinion it makes the poem very difficult to understand – I do not think that a reader easily understands that "O that none ever loved . . ." is spoken, and I shd wish to put a dash at end of line before it, or to set it in inverted commas or print it in italic. I want to distinguish it in some way.

Also I think that delicate-stepping should be hyphened and in (8) "The cloths of heaven," I shd like to change the punctuation very much.

Please tell me what you wd wish.

In my quotations from the English poets I find that I have most from Shelley: but some of them are mere scraps. Then comes Shakespeare with 32. These of course include some sonnets and nearly all his lyrics. Then Milton with 26.* Keats with 18 and Blake and you are about equal.

Elizabeth, who has assisted me very competently is pleased with the book, and some very seriously-minded friends of mine are enthusiastic: so I hope it may have something of the effect that I desire. I am extremely grateful to you for your willingness to allow me to use your work — it was essential to me — and a chief part of my pleasure in the book is my belief that it will triumphantly justify the more imaginative poetry. I am now only waiting to get hold of a suitable type: it is hard to find one.

We enjoyed your visit immensely, and hope that you will come again — Elizabeth was of course much encouraged by your praise of her poems.

I have not yet attacked Macmillan about Tagore. I shall come up to London & interview him.

With many thanks for the books.

Yours ever
R B

*Two or three of these are prose

From ROBERT BRIDGES   Chilswell, near Oxford
MS Bridges   [12 July] 1915

[This letter is misdated 'June 12' by Bridges.]

My dear Yeats,

You are overwhelming me with gifts. The Gods & fighting men have arrived. Reading the preface I thought wonderfully well of Lady Gregory until I got to the last page of it and saw your name at the bottom.

I am coming up to town on Thursday & leave on Friday. As I am engaged to lunch on Friday I fear that I may not see you. I had intended to tackle Sir Fredk Macmillan about Tagore's poems but find to my disgust that he is not in town: so I must put that business off.

I shall be staying with L Pearsall Smith, 11 Leonard's Terrace, Chelsea. I can't tell what my engagements may be

Yours ever
R B

From W. B. YEATS   Chilswell, near Oxford
MS Bridges   [13 July 1915]

[T. Sturge Moore (1870–1944) designed many of Yeats's
book-covers. The Reverend Charles Feer Andrews (1871–
1940) had joined Tagore's Institution in Santiniketan in
1913. In his letter to Rothenstein on 4 April 1915, Tagore
had commented that 'Andrews does not admire the alterations made by Bridges but that does not affect me' (IE 195),
but both Edward J. Thompson (1886–1946) and Rothenstein agreed with Yeats (see IE 182 n.9).]

Dear Bridges
    I have not written because I have mislaid your last letter
but one & have been hoping to find it again. I chiefly
remember you asked me about my stops & commas. Do what
you will. I do not understand stops. I write my work so
completely for the ear that I feel helpless when I have to
measure pauses by stops & commas.
    I have been looking through Sturge Moore for poems to
draw your attention to. Read "Kindness" in "Poems" (Duck-
worth 1906) & the "Dying Swan" and "Semele" in "The Sea
is Kind" (Grant Richards 1914)[.] There are other beautiful
things but much that is too loose and easy.
    If you wish it I could call on you Friday or meet you
anywhere, but I expect you will not have time.
                                    Yours
                                    W B YEATS

    I heard from Binyon a week ago that Rothenstein had
told him of the difficulty with Tagore about your book.
Andrews is the mischief maker. I have written Rothenstein an
urgent letter & suggested his sending it to Tagore but have
not heard from Rothenstein.
    I wish I could see more of your daughters work. I have
read out the best of what I have to a number of people.

From ROBERT BRIDGES   Chilswell, near Oxford
MS Bridges   [14 July 1915]

[Bridges probably refers to Tagore's letter of 19 June 1915,
in which he wrote 'I am sorry to find that my publishers did
not see their way to grant you permission to include in your
anthology the Gitanjali in its altered form. My hesitation is
chiefly owing to my sentiment of gratitude to Yeats who
edited these forms and I feel it would be showing want of
loyalty to him if I allowed any alteration in any of them. At
least I ought to be quite certain that he approves of it'
(BL 35).]

My dear Yeats,
        Providence has summoned Sir Frederick Macmillan to
town, so that I shall see him on Friday morning after all. I
really expect him to come round, and may find your letter to
me useful. There can be no objection to my showing it to
him in confidence. But if you object to his reading "Andrews
in the mischief-maker" send a line to me at Pearsall Smith's
(11 St. Leonard's Terrace, Chelsea) and it will be in time to
stop me. My appointment with Macmillan is 10.45 on Friday
morning, & I lunch at the Temple at 1.0. There will no doubt
be a gap between – but Macmillan's is the E end or rather the
City, so that there might not be time to make it worth while
to go round to Woburn Buildings. I shall fill up the time in
the city. I do not think that I have anything special to talk
about, and I go off on Saturday forenoon. My wife is coming
up and I meet her and go with her to lunch at Epping where
my son is with his regiment, and has a spare afternoon.
        But I think I will be at the Savile Club in Piccadilly at
5 p.m. Friday. I ought to go there – and there you will find
me if you are in those parts and can look in.
                                        Yours ever
                                        R B

P.S. The afternoon post brings me an engagement wh' I must
not miss for Friday 4–5, so that it is unlikely that I shall be

at the Savile at any rate before 5.30.

Also it brings a letter from Tagore which will I think finish off Macmillan.

I have reopened the letter to add this.

From ROBERT BRIDGES   Chilswell, near Oxford
MS Bridges   26 July [1915]

[Bridges means to refer to poem No. 67 in *Gitanjali*. He has marked the second sentence in this letter 'Private'. Tagore responded to Bridges' letter on 19 August 1915, saying 'as for my own opinion I think there is a stage in all writings where they must have a finality in spite of their short-comings. Authors have their limitations and we have to put up with them if they give us something positively good. If we begin to think of improvement there is no end to it and differences of opinion are sure to arise. . . . Flaws are there but life makes up for all its flaws' (BL 40). Earlier, on 13 August 1915, Tagore had written to his publishers, explaining 'If my instinct is right then I think the versions of trans-lations that are already before the public should never be published in altered forms — otherwise they would lose all idea of finality and many a reader's mind would be exercised in trying to improve them. But as I was not quite sure whether Dr. Bridges' taking liberty with only one of my poems would matter much I wanted to depend upon your discretion' (BL 38).

Harold Cox (1859–1936), a Liberal M.P., was appar-ently arranging a tribute for the birthday on 10 September of the Prime Minister, Herbert Henry Asquith (1852–1928).]

My dear Yeats,

Macmillan has after all refused to allow me to print my version of Gitanjali 69 "Thou art the sky." It seems that he had definite instructions from Tagore, wh¨ were contra-dictory of his expressions of willingness to me.

No doubt he was unwilling to offend me by refusing,

and therefore put the thing off on to Macmillan.

I have just despatched to Tagore a long letter, which I think will bring him round: but I shd be glad if you sent him a line also. I suppose he is at Bolpur. He wrote to me that his only or main scruple was the fear of offending you after what you had done to help him.

About the meeting on Harold Cox's business. I feel that it may be expected of me that I shd attend the meeting, which I think is this week. On the other hand I do not see that any good wd come of it, so that I shall not go. I am writing to [the] Secretary to tell him that I cannot sign the petition or memorial to Asquith. The intention is very good but I do not see that there is any machinery for carrying it out successfully.

Yours ever

R B

I am writing to your publishers for leave to print your things, and have identified publishers of all but "O hurry where by water among trees' which is on p 150 of Tauchnitz. Can you remember what publisher holds this one? I shd like to know.

From W. B. YEATS	Coole Park
MS Bridges	1 August 1915

[Yeats had written to Tagore on 31 July 1915: 'I should be sorry to prevent Robert Bridges from making the slight changes he wishes. He is at moments a most admirable poet and always the chief scholar in English style now living. His creative power is not great though very exquisite but no living man is so well fitted to measure and emend a detail of [speech?]. I have the same mother tongue that he has, but I would be grateful should he care to revise a poem of mine, certainly I would be ashamed if consideration for my revision should keep you from accepting his. I feel that he is the head of my craft in England and have felt so since the death of

Swinburne, or from before it for ʒwinburne's abundant genius repelled me' (IE 212 n.1). Yeats's letter succeeded, and on 31 August 1915 Tagore wrote to his publisher: 'I am just in receipt of a letter from Yeats, strongly recommending me to allow Dr. Bridges to use in his anthology the Gitanjali poem with the alterations. As I feel I cannot refuse Yeats I shall be happy if you see your way to granting his request and send your permission to Dr. Bridges' (BL 42).

Yeats's play was *At the Hawk's Well*, first performed on 2 April 1916.]

My dear Mr Bridges

I have written to Tagore; I wrote a couple of days ago & hope we have prevailed.

"O hurry where by water among trees" is a late re-writing of a poem published by Bullen. I imagine you should write to him. The amended poem is only in Tauchnitz so for this you need no leave but mine.

Tell your daughter that the other day Lady Gregory who was dining with me, took up while waiting for me — I had gone out to post a letter — your daughters poems. I had not told her of them & she found them herself & read them with admiration. I have made Sturge Moore very enthusiastic about them.

I shall be here till September I imagine. It is my one chance of finishing a new play.

Yours
W B YEATS

From ROBERT BRIDGES   Chilswell, near Oxford
MS Bridges   7 October [1915]

[In a note to one of his selections from Shelley's *Prometheus Unbound* (3.3.44–62), Bridges explained that 'The great beauty of this passage suffers from the involved grammar, which deepens its obscurities, while the original punctuation still further hampers it. I have entirely discarded Shelley's punctuation and added some capitals, hoping to make a more readable text.'

An annotation in Bridges's copy of *Gitanjali* indicates that the 'two critics' were John Alexander Stewart (1846–1933), Professor of Philosophy at Oxford, and Henry Bradley (1845–1923), a philologist and one of the co-founders of the Society for Pure English. Bridges's changes in Tagore's poem amount to virtual rewriting. In *Gitanjali* the poem reads

Thou art the sky and thou art the nest as well.

O thou beautiful, there in the nest it is thy
love that encloses the soul with colours and sounds
and odours.

There comes the morning with the golden basket in
her right hand bearing the wreath of beauty, silently
to crown the earth.

And there comes the evening over the lonely meadows
deserted by herds, through trackless paths, carrying
cool draughts of peace in her golden pitcher from the
western ocean of rest.

But there, where spreads the infinite sky for the
soul to take her flight in, reigns the stainless white
radiance. There is no day nor night, nor form nor
colour, and never, never a word.

In *The Spirit of Man* this becomes

Thou art the sky and Thou art also the nest.

O Thou Beautiful! how in the nest thy love embraceth
the soul with sweet sounds and colour and fragrant
odours!

Morning cometh there, bearing in her golden basket the
wreath of beauty, silently to crown the earth.

And there cometh Evening, o'er lonely meadows deserted
of the herds, by trackless ways, carrying in her
golden pitcher cool draughts of peace from the
ocean-calms of the west.

But where thine infinite sky spreadeth for the soul to
take her flight, a stainless white radiance reigneth;

wherein is neither day nor night, nor form nor colour,
nor ever any word.

In his note Bridges explained 'I have to thank him [Tagore]
and his English publisher for allowing me to quote from this
book, and in the particular instance of this very beautiful
poem, for the author's friendliness in permitting me to shift a
few words for the sake of what I considered more effective
rhythm or grammar.'

Bridges's son, Edward Bridges (1892–1959), survived
the war to serve in the British Service and eventually became
Chancellor of Reading University.]

My dear Yeats,

I am now returning you Rabi's letter. I am very much
obliged to you for writing to him: and I am sure that your
appeal was the most powerful of all my machinations. He
wrote also to Macmillan and to me, and this morning I got
two letters from India telling me a great deal of how he is
going on.

I ought to have written to you before, but you asked me
to write to London where you said you wd be returning in a
fortnight. I am afraid it may be more than a fortnight ago,
but I can't tell. What sets me writing today is that my wife
has fallen suddenly ill: and the consequence is that I am not
able to settle down to anything. The book is going on well
and I am just beginning to pass final revises. I have found all
sorts of difficulties that I didn't foresee. For instance yester-
day I had to repunctuate a piece of Shelley's Prometheus, 19
lines. It was nonsense in the received text, or at least
unintelligible and I made 13 changes in stops etc in the 19
lines, arriving at something presentable. I consulted the MS at
the Bodleian Library, and found that Shelleys own punctuation was almost worse than nothing.

Tagore in his letter to me showed such reluctance that
when I read it I determined at first to let him have his way.
But I tried my version of the poem again with two critics.
One of them knew the Gitanjali well and had never remarked

this particular poem (which I hold to be the best of all) till he saw it in my version. The other man was quite a stranger to Tagore's poems, & admired my version very much indeed. He is as good and severe a judge as one could find – and then when I showed him Tagore's version he said that it betrayed its unacquaintance with English idiom: and that he thought he shd not have been much struck by it, tho' after seeing my version he could not of course judge very well. This decided me, and I am sure Tagore will not repent of his consent.

I have a long envelope now full of the correspondence on this matter, & I am sorry to say it does not do R T much credit. As far as I can make out he has ruined his reputation with his countrymen, while this man who has taken him in charge must be stuffing him with vanity and making an ass of him. Everyone says that his last visit to England ruined him. I hope I shall be writing again to you ere long. But my boy is at the front in the trenches in France, and I can't tell what may happen.

Yours ever

R B

I was much touched by your inscription in the Tauchnitz.

From ROBERT BRIDGES   Chilswell, near Oxford
MS Bridges   12 October [1915]

[Bridges is referring to the 1895 *Poems* text of 'The Sad Shepherd'. In *The Spirit of Man* Bridges used a colon after 'comforting' and 'whorls' for 'whirls', noting 'two misprints corrected'. In fact, Yeats had reinserted the comma of the first two printings after 'comforting' in the 1904 revision of *Poems*; the change was overlooked in the 1906 *Poetical Works* but was included in all later printings. Yeats never used 'whorls'.]

My dear Yeats,
    I am correcting proofs, & I have just come to your man whom sorrow named his friend & I find in your first book in the last 6 lines
        (1) no stop at *comforting*
        (2) last line *"Among her widening whirls, forgetting him"*
I want a colon (?) at comforting and I have no doubt that you mean *whorls* for *whirls*. It may have been a misprint. Whirl I think always implies motion, & whorl seems the correct word. I shall print both these corrections unless I hear from you. (Of course I shd note them if I do not get your authority.[)] If I get that I shall note "two misprints corrected.["]
                                        Yours ever
                                        R B

I noted whorls for whirls in margin of your bk when I first read it — as a misprint.

From W. B. YEATS   London
MS Bridges   18 October [1915]

[On this letter Bridges has noted 'No 1ll text', referring to 'The Sad Shepherd' in *The Spirit of Man*.]

My dear Bridges:
    Do exactly what you like & forgive my delay in answering. You are entirely right & may call them "Misprints" or anything else you please.
    I wonder if your informant is right about Tagore. At half a dozen times in the last twenty years my own fellow countrymen would have said (& always when I was most right) that I had lost their confidence. The position of a man of letters in a patriotic movement is always very difficult. I noticed that Tagore went back from Europe with increased confidence & wondered if there would not be trouble. I

thought that when he met his old enemies he would probably make himself disagreeable.

Yours
W B YEATS

From ROBERT BRIDGES   Chilswell, near Oxford
MS Bridges   2 December [1915?]

[The dating of this letter is based on the fact that Yeats presented a lecture on 'The Irish Theatre' at Sunderland House in London on 6 December 1915. Also, his letter to Bridges of 18 October 1915 had been written from the Royal Societies Club; the lost letter to which Bridges is replying may have been written from the Savile Club, or possibly Bridges is confusing the two clubs. In his letter, Yeats must have waived the fees for the inclusion of his poems in *The Spirit of Man* and urged that his gesture be kept private.]

My dear Yeats,
        It is very gracious of you to make this concession, & since it involves you in further trouble I feel sorry that I have led you into it: but I suppose it had now better go on. Perhaps after all they may find that they can do without the remission[.]
        I wish I could be in town and hear some of your lectures: and I now much regret that I did not manage to make more of your time in Oxford, but you were so often away: and I did not foresee that you wd shake the dust of Oxford from your feet so soon.
        This with my best thanks to you at the Savile. I am afraid I shan't be up in town until you have left it.
        I will enforce the need of secrecy on my daughter[.]
Yours ever
R B

From W. B. YEATS   London
MS Bridges   13 June [1916]

[Yeats refers to the Easter Rebellion in Dublin from 24 to 30
April 1916. The 'friend' is Maud Gonne (1866–1953).]

Dear Bridges:
    Please forgive me for not having answered your letter of
May 12. All my habits of thought and work were upset by
this tragic Irish rebellion which has swept away friends &
fellow workers. I have just returned from Dublin where of
course one talks of nothing else, & now, if I can get a
passport I must go to a friend in Normandy who has been
greatly troubled by it all. But for this I would have gone to
you & had indeed, before you wrote, intended to suggest
myself as a visitor. I thank you very much.
                                        Yours
                                        W B YEATS

From ROBERT BRIDGES   Chilswell, near Oxford
MS Bridges   2 December [1922]

[John C. Squire (1884–1958) was a poet and critic.]

My dear Yates,
    If you have nothing to do next Sunday in town would
you spend your weekend with us? If you cannot leave earlier
there is a good train from Paddington at 4.45. I wd meet you
at Oxford Station – and there are very good trains back on
Monday morning.
    What made me think of this was that we had a visitor
today who is in active pursuit of you. Squire introduced him
to me. He is a young American: and will be staying some
time on this Hill. He said that you had written to him as if
you wd be able to see him later on in Dublin. Wherever you
are I can promise you that he will seek you out. He seems a

profound student of your work and a reverent worshipper. If you come I will ask him to lunch.

We are alone now, my wife, Elizabeth and myself, and you wd give us great pleasure and wd do us all three much good if you wd come as I suggest.

Of course the earlier on Saty the better, & you need bring no changes of raiment that you do not wish to wear.

It wd be convenient if you wd write as soon as you can whether you can come, and your admirer wd make other plans for Sunday if he cannot meet you here.

Also say if there is anyone in Oxford you wd like to meet – I could send him or them (or her) an invitat for Sunday.

> Yours ever
> R BRIDGES

From W. B. YEATS   Dublin
MS Bridges   4 January [1923]

[Yeats became a member of the Irish Senate on 11 December 1922.]

My dear Bridges:
  I have just found a letter of yours dated Dec 2 stuffed into the hollow place between the arm & the cushions of a leather arm-chair. I wonder if I ever answered – to the best of my belief it only reached me here after my return from England. I have in fact been looking in vain through my letters because of an uncertain idea that I had some unanswered letter from you. If it was really unanswered please forgive me. When I got back here I found myself a senator & the senate, though it did not break in upon my morning hours when I write verse etc took away a large part of those afternoon hours when I write letters. I wish very much I could have gone to you & heaven knows when I shall be in England – probably not till peace has been made. Life

here is interesting, but restless & unsafe – I have two bullet holes through my windows – as it must always be when the sheep endevour to controll the goats who are by nature so much the more enterprising race.

Yes I know the young American by letter I think. He has the American passion for ideas, combined, I judge, with the American intellectual indolence and physical energy. He will probably reach me sooner or later – in one letter he threatened to come to Co Galway. His mother, when with child with him, probably listened to fifteen lectures a week, two a day including Sundays which is quite moderate in New York.

Yours
W B YEATS

From ROBERT BRIDGES   Chilswell, near Oxford
MS Bridges   8 December 1929

[Bridges's poem was *The Testament of Beauty*, published on 24 October 1929. *The Trembling of the Veil* was published in October 1922. Yeats had married Georgie Hyde-Lees (1892–1968) on 20 October 1917; their children were Anne (1919–   ) and Michael (1921–   ).]

My dear Yeats

I am sending you a copy of my new poem. I shd have sent it before but there was a rush at the Press, and my conveniences were overlooked. I send it because I shd be very sorry not to send it, so that the gratification is on my side complete, & I ask for no acknowledgment. I have been very sorry to have seen nothing of you for so long, and as a consequence I have seen nothing of your work since "The lifting of the Veil" of which I am glad to possess a copy.

I hope you keep well, and enjoy yr share of Irish politics. There is a great glut of disturbances so great that there is even a hope it will be sufficient to teach many fools wisdom – I mean not real wisdom, but fatigue of folly.

We send kindest remembrances & love to you & Mrs. Yeats who I hope is well, and to offspring – a convenient word in my ignorance of detail

Yours ever
ROBERT BRIDGES

From W. B. YEATS *to*
MRS. ROBERT BRIDGES   Rapallo, Italy
MS Bridges   7 May[1930]

[Bridges had died on 21 April 1930. The 'great house' was probably Garsington, the home of Lady Ottoline Violet Anne Morrell (1873–1938) and her husband Philip (1870–1943).]

Dear Mrs. Bridges,

May I, despite the slightness of our acquaintance, tell how much I feel your great loss. I think I remember your husband most clearly, as I saw him at some great house near you where there were Servian delegates. He came through the undistinguished crowd, an image of mental and physical perfection, & one of the Servians turned to me in obvious excitement to ask his name. He has always seemed the only poet, whose influence has always heightened & purified the art of others & all who write with deliberation are his debtors.

My wife joins with me in sending you our sympathy.

Yours
W B YEATS

Appendix A: Yeats's 'Mr. Robert Bridges'

[The text is from *The Bookman* (London) for June 1897.
When Yeats published a revised version of the article as '*The
Return of Ulysses*' in *Ideas of Good and Evil* (1903), he
omitted most of the third paragraph, all of the fifth through
seventh paragraphs, and the postscript. The later text was
included with minor changes in Volume VI of the *Collected
Works in Verse & Prose* (1908), *Essays* (1924), and *Essays
and Introductions* (1961).]

LIVING POETS.

IV. – Mr. Robert Bridges.

M. Maeterlinck, in his beautiful "Treasure of the Humble,"
compares the dramas of our stage to the paintings of an
obsolete taste; and the dramas of the stage, for which he
hopes, to the paintings of a taste that cannot become
obsolete.[1] "The true artist," he says, "no longer chooses
Marius triumphing over the Cimbrians, or the assassination of
the Duke of Guise, as fit subjects for his art; for he is well
aware that the psychology of victory or murder is but
elementary and exceptional, and that the solemn voice of
men and things, the voice that issues forth so timidly and
hesitatingly, cannot be heard amidst the idle uproar of acts of
violence. And therefore will he place on his canvas a house
lost in the heart of the country, a door open at the end of a
passage, a face or hands at rest."[2] I do not understand him to
mean that our dramas should have no victories or murders,

51

for he quotes for our example plays that have both,[3] but only that their victories and murders shall not be to excite our nerves, but to illustrate the reveries of a wisdom which shall be as much a part of the daily life of the wise as a face or hands at rest[.] And certainly the greater plays of the past ages have been built after such a fashion. If this fashion is about to become our fashion also, and there are signs that it is, plays like the plays of Mr. Robert Bridges will come suddenly out of that obscurity into which all poetry, that is not lyrical poetry, has fallen, and even popular criticism will begin to know something about them. Some day the few among us, who care for poetry more than any temporal thing, and who believe that its delights cannot be perfect when we read it alone in our rooms and long for one to share in its delights, but that they might be perfect in the theatre, when we share them friend with friend, lover with beloved, will persuade a few idealists to seek out the lost art of speaking, and seek out ourselves the lost art, that is perhaps nearest of all arts to eternity, the subtle art of listening. When that day comes we will talk much of Mr. Bridges; for did he not write scrupulous, passionate poetry to be sung and to be spoken, when there were few to sing and as yet none to speak? There is one play especially, "The Return of Ulysses," which we will praise for perfect after its kind, the kind of our new drama of wisdom, for it moulds into dramatic shape, and with as much as possible of literal translation, those closing books of the Odyssey which are perhaps the most perfect poetry of the world, and compels that great tide of song to flow through delicate dramatic verse, with little abatement of its own leaping and clamorous speed. As I read, the gathering passion overwhelms me, as it did when Homer himself was the singer, and when I read at last the lines in which the maid describes to Penelope the battle with the suitors, at which she looks through the open door, I tremble with excitement.

"*Penelope*: Alas! what cries! Say, is the prince still safe?
The Maid: He shieldeth himself well, and striketh surely;

His foes fall down before him. Ah! now what can I see?
Who cometh? Lo! a dazzling helm, a spear
Of silver or electron; sharp and swift
The piercings. How they fall! Ha! shields are raised
In vain. I am blinded, or the beggar-man
Hath waxed in strength. He is changed, he is young, O
    strange!
He is all in golden armour. These are gods
That slay the suitors. (*Runs to Penelope.*) O lady,
    forgive me.
'Tis Aɪes' self. I saw his crispèd beard;
I saw beneath his helm his curlèd locks."[4]

The coming of Athene helmed "in silver or electron"
and her transformation of Ulysses are not, as the way is with
the only modern dramas that popular criticism holds to be
dramatic, the climax of an excitement of the nerves, but of
that unearthly excitement whose fruit is wisdom, and which
is of like kind with the ecstasy of the seers, an altar flame,
unshaken by the winds of the world, and burning every
moment with whiter and purer brilliance.

The other eight plays have not this gathering passion,
but they have much beauty, and much beauty even that
might be a delight upon the stage if we had but possessed our
lost arts for a little while and grown easy in their use.[5]
"Prometheus, the Fire Bringer," "Nero: the First Part," and
"Palicio" are early work, and, with the exception of the first,
which is vigourous and simple, though a little slow in its
motion, they appear to me rather loose in their hold on
character and incident, and, with the exception of
"Prometheus, the Fire Bringer," do not move me greatly.
"The Christian Captives," which followed "The Return of
Ulysses," and "The Humours of the Court," and "Nero: the
Second Part" are, like "Nero: the First Part" and "Palicio,"
in a more or less Shakesperean manner; and though excellent
critics consider "Nero: the Second Part" Mr. Bridges' best
play, and though I find much beauty in all and great beauty

in it, I prefer Mr. Bridges when he follows a more or less classical model, as he does in "The Feast of Bacchus," which is, however, less a poem than an admirable farce condensed from "Terence":

> "Or some Terentian play
> Renew, whose excellent
> Adjusted folds betray
> How once Menander went";[6]

and in "Achilles in Scyros" – a placid and charming setting for many placid and charming lyrics:

> "And ever we keep a feast of delight
> The betrothal of hearts, when spirits unite,
> Creating an offspring of joy, a treasure
> Unknown to the bad, for whom
> The gods foredoom
> The glitter of pleasure
> And a dark tomb."[7]

The poet who writes best in the Shakesperean manner is a poet with a circumstantial and instinctive mind, who delights to speak with strange voices and to see his mind in the mirror of Nature; while Mr. Bridges, like most of us to-day, has a lyrical and meditative mind, and delights to speak with his own voice and to see Nature in the mirror of his mind. In reading his plays in a Shakesperean manner, I find that he is constantly arranging his story in such and such a way because he has read that the persons he is writing of did such and such things, and not because his soul has passed into the soul of their world and understood its unchangeable destinies. His "Return of Ulysses" is a triumph of beauty, because its classical gravity of speech, which does not, like Shakespeare's verse, desire the vivacity of common life, purifies and subdues all passion into lyrical and meditative ecstasies, and because the unity of place and time in the late acts compels a logical rather than instinctive procession of incidents; and if the Shakesperean "Nero: Second Part" approaches it in beauty and in dramatic power, it is because it eddies about Nero and Seneca, who had both, to a great extent, lyrical and meditative minds. Had Mr. Bridges been a true Shakesperian, the pomp and glory of the world would have drowned that subtle voice that speaks amid our heterogeneous lives of a life lived in obedience to a lonely and distinguished ideal.

"The Return of Ulysses" and "Achilles in Scyros" move me the most of Mr. Bridges' longer poems, and after them, and I think before the "Nero: Second Part," I number "Eros and Psyche," in which the part that comes closest to folk lore, the description of the tasks that Aphrodite sets to Psyche, is particularly moving:

> Then Psyche said: "This is the biting flood
> Of black Cocytus, silvered with the gleam
> Of souls, that guilty of another's blood
> Are pent therein, and as they swim they scream."[8]

I cannot judge properly of "Eden: an Oratorio," and of the "Purcell Commemoration Ode," and of the little I have seen of "The Yattingdon Hymnal," for they must be judged with the music, and I have no knowledge of music.[9] I find the little I have seen of the Hymnal full of intellectual passion; and "Eden," which does not, and I know not well why, greatly move me when I read it as a poem, has, when I imagine it as sung, a curious dramatic ecstasy, particularly in such things as the repeated "And what is man?" at the opening. These poems, except possibly the Hymnal, of which I cannot yet judge, however, seem to me of a less accomplished rhythm and easy beauty than the poems in the "Shorter Poems" which are written to be read only.[10] Mr. Bridges has a more assured mastery over the theory and practice of a various and subtle rhythm of words than any living poet, and though his poems for music are honourable deeds, his poems are at their best when free from the bondage of any rhythm but the rhythm of words. Had he to remember the rhythm of a tune he could not, it is probable, have written.

> But, ah! the leaves of summer that lie on the
>   ground!
> What havoc! The laughing timbrels of June,
> That curtained the birds' cradles, and screened
>   their song,
> That sheltered the cooing birds at noon,
> Of airy fans the delicate throng –
> Torn and scattered around!
> Far out afield they lie,
> In the watery furrows die,
> In the grassy pools of the flood they sink and
>   drown,
> Green-golden, orange, vermilion, golden and
>   brown,
> The high year's flaunting crown,
> Shattered and trampled down.
>
> The day is done; the tired land looks for night;
> She prays to the night to keep
> In peace her nerves of delight:
> While silver mist upstealeth silently,
> And the broad cloud-driving moon in the clear sky
> Lifts o'er the firs her shining shield
> And in her tranquil light
> Sleep falls on forest and field.
> See! sleep hath fallen; the trees are asleep;
> The night is come. The land is wrapt in sleep.[11]

I know of no poet of our time, and few of our century, who can so perfectly knead thought and rhythm into the one mystical body of faint flame. Who can say whether the charm of these verses, the first three in one of his early lyrics, is in their thought or in their rhythm?

> I heard a linnet courting
>   His lady in the spring;
> His mates were idly sporting,
>   Nor stayed to hear him sing
>   His song of love.
> I fear my speech distorting
>   His tender love.
>
> The phrases of his pleading
>   Were full of young delight;
> And she that gave him heeding
>   Interpreted aright
>   His gay—sweet notes—
> So sadly marred in the reading—
>   His tender notes.
>
> And when he ceased, the hearer
>   Awaited the refrain,
> Till swiftly perching nearer
>   He sang his song again,
>   His pretty song:—
> Would that my verse spake fitter
>   His tender song.[1][2]

The more a poet rids his verses of heterogeneous knowledge and irrelevant analysis, the more he purifies his mind with elaborate art, the more does the little ritual of his verse resemble the great ritual of nature, and become mysterious and inscrutable. He becomes, as all the great mystics have believed, a vessel of the creative power of God; and whether he be a great poet or a small poet, we can praise the poems, which but seem to be his, with the extremity of praise that we give this great ritual which is but copied from the same eternal model. There is poetry that is like the white light of noon, and poetry that has the heaviness of woods, and poetry that has the golden light of dawn or of sunset; and I find in the poetry of Mr. Bridges the pale colours, the delicate silence, the low murmurs of cloudy country days, when the plough is in the earth, and the clouds darkening towards sunset; and had I the great gift of praising, I would praise it as I would praise these things.

W. B. YEATS.

P.S.–It is a common idea that Mr. Bridges' poems are published privately, and are not in the market. They can all be bought cheaply enough from Messrs. George Bell and Sons.

NOTES TO APPENDIX A

1. Maurice Maeterlinck, *The Treasure of the Humble*, trans. Alfred Sutro, intro. A. B. Walkley (April 1897), later reviewed by Yeats in *The Bookman* for July 1897. Yeats has misread a passage of 'The Tragical in Daily Life' in which Maeterlinck compares the inferior drama of the present age to sculpture: 'and truly one may say that anachronism dominates the stage, and that dramatic art dates back as many years as the art of sculpture. Far different it is with the other arts – with painting and music, for instance – for these have learned to select and reproduce those obscurer phases of daily life that are not the less deep-rooted and amazing' (p. 101).
2. *The Treasure of the Humble*, pp. 101–102; 'a door open' for 'an open door'.
3. Maeterlinck refers to *King Lear*, *Macbeth*, and *Hamlet*, as well as several classical tragedies.
4. *The Return of Ulysses* (1890), V.2686–97. With changes in punctuation, 'Maid' for '2nd Maid', 'can I see' for 'see I', 'suitors' for 'wooers', and 'curlèd' for 'curling'.
5. The other works gathered in *Eight Plays* are *Nero: Part I*

(1885), *The Feast of Bacchus* (1889), *Palicio* (1890), *The Christian Captives* (1890), *Achilles in Scyros* (1890), *The Humours of the Court* (1893), and *Nero: Part 2* (1894).

6. From stanza nine of 'Spring. Ode II. Reply," first published in *Poems* (1879) and included in *Poems* (1884) and *Shorter Poems* (1890). The quotations marks around 'Terence' are doubtless a compositor's error.

7. *Achilles in Scyros*, 1594–1600; with changes in punctuation.

8. From stanza six of 'January' in *Eros and Psyche*, revised edition (1894); with a change in punctuation and 'silvered' for 'silver'd'. In the first edition (1885) 'January' was called 'Measure 11'.

9. *Eden: an Oratorio* (1891); *Ode for the Bicentenary Commemoration of Henry Purcell* (1896); *The Yattendon Hymnal* (1895–99).

10. *Shorter Poems*, Books I–IV (1890); *Book V* (Daniel Press, 1893; George Bell, 1894).

11. The last two stanzas of No. 23 in Book IV of the *Shorter Poems*; with changes in punctuation and lacking the stress on 'Sée' and 'sléep' in the penultimate line.

12. The first three stanzas of No. 5 in Book I of the *Shorter Poems*; with changes in punctuation. The poem was first published in *Poems* (1873), revised for the 1890 *Shorter Poems*, and further revised for the fourth edition of *Shorter Poems* (1894); Yeats follows the latter text.

Appendix B: Yeats volumes in Bridges's library

The books, listed in chronological order, are in the possession of the Bridges family. References are to Allan Wade, *A Bibliography of the Writings of W. B. Yeats*, 3rd ed., rev. Russell K. Alspach (London: Rupert Hart-Davis, 1968).

1. *The Celtic Twilight*. London: Lawrence and Bullen, 1893. Wade 8 (first issue).
     Bridges has objected to the phrase 'turned up' in 'The Sorcerers'.
2. *Poems*. London: T. Fisher Unwin, 1895. Wade 15.
     On the flyleaf Bridges has noted 'I never saw any of Yeats' poems till I bought this book recommended to me by MacKail'. The book is heavily marked throughout. For instance, Bridges has noted the repetition in the poems of such words as 'sigh', 'glimmer', 'sad', 'pearl', 'white', 'gray', 'dim', 'soft', 'old', 'pale', 'faint', 'fade', and 'weary'. He has suggested deletions in 'The Wanderings of Oisin' and *The Countess Cathleen*. Elsewhere he has queried individual words or images.
3. *The Secret Rose*. London: Lawrence and Bullen, 1897. Wade 21.
     Numerous markings on matters on detail through 'The Curse of Hanrahan the Red', but only one comment thereafter.
4. *The Wind Among the Reeds*. Second edition. London: Elkin Mathews, 1899. Wade 27 (first and second editions issued simultaneously).
     Inscribed on the flyleaf 'Robert Bridges from W. B. Yeats. 1899.' Below the inscription Bridges has noted

'The pencil corrections by W.B.Y.' Five of Yeats's corrections are among those included on an errata slip in later copies of this edition; the changes were made in the third edition (1900). Yeats's other correction, 'blossom' for 'blossoms' in line 21 of 'Michael Robartes asks Forgiveness because of his Many Moods' (as in *The Saturday Review*, 2 November 1895), was neither included on the errata slip nor made in any of the later editions.

5. Rabindranath Tagore, *Gitanjali*. Introduction by W. B. Yeats. London: Macmillan, 1913. Wade 264.

On the flyleaf Bridges has noted: 'These poems were selected by W.B.Y. out of an immense mass of MS. Yeats made hardly any alterations in the English. Rabi said of himself that he had always been an unpopular poet, & that the Bengalis regarded him as difficult to understand: and he felt his countrymen's neglect of him. He thought that the English recognised their poets much better than the Indians did: & that we had a better literary tradition & respect for poetry. This view he got no doubt from the limitation of his intercourse in England: it was chiefly among literary people that he went.'

On top of the pages containing No. 67 ('Thou art the sky') Bridges has written: 'Prof Stewart cannot remember having remarked this [–] read mine thought it splendid. H.B. says he was attracted by my version, but after read orig. & said he was not sure that he wd have observed it. He felt it is not quite English idiom.'

6. *Responsibilities*. Dundrum: Cuala Press, 1914. Wade 110.

No markings.

7. *Reveries Over Childhood & Youth*. London: Macmillan, 1916. Wade 113.

No markings.

8. *The Trembling of the Veil*. London: T. Werner Laurie, 1922. Wade 133.

Presented to Bridges by Schuyler B. Jackson.
9. *Autobiographies.* London: Macmillan, 1926. Wade 151. Bridges has marked various passages throughout most of the book. Many of the pages in 'The Stirring of the Bones' are uncut.

In 1915 Yeats sent Bridges copies of Wade 101, *The Green Helmet* (New York: Macmillan, 1912), and Wade 103, *A Selection from the Poetry of W. B. Yeats* (Leipzig: Bernhard Tauchnitz, 1913); but these are no longer part of the Bridges library.

Appendix C: Bridges volumes in Yeats's library

The books, listed in chronological order, are in the possession of Miss Anne Yeats. References are to George L. McKay, *A Bibliography of Robert Bridges* (New York: Columbia University Press; London: Oxford University Press, 1933).

1. *The Christian Captives: A Tragedy in Five Acts in a Mixed Manner*. London: Edward Bumpus, 1890. McKay 17.
    Pages uncut except for 124–6.
2. *The Shorter Poems*. London: Geo Bell & Sons, 1890. McKay 19a.
    Inscribed 'W. B. Yeats 1890 November 1st.' Yeats has made the two corrections noted on the errata slip: 'empty tomb' to 'airy tomb' in Book II, No. 13, and 'shattered trees' to 'shattered the trees' in Book IV, No. 23. The pencil sketch on p. 36 is possibly by Yeats.
3. *Achilles in Scyros*. London: Geo. Bell & Sons, 1892. Not in McKay.
    No markings.
4. *Eros & Psyche*. Revised edition. London: George Bell and Sons, 1894. McKay 27.
    No markings.
5. *Ode for the Bicentenary Commemoration of Henry Purcell*. London: Elkin Mathews, 1896. McKay 31.
    No markings.
6. *Poems Written in the Year MCMXIII*. Printed by St. John Hornby at the Ashendene Press, Shelley House, Chelsea, for Robert Bridges, Poet Laureate, in the month of December of the year 1914. McKay 47.
    No markings.

7. *The Spirit of Man: An Anthology in English & French From the Philosophers & Poets.* London: Longmans Green & Co, 1916. McKay 105.

> No markings.

8. *Poems of Gerard Manley Hopkins.* Edited with notes by Robert Bridges. London: Humphrey Milford, 1918. McKay 117.

> Inscribed 'T.W.B.Y. from J.Q. Jan 28, 1920.' No markings.

9. *The Chilswell Book of English Poetry.* Compiled & annotated for the use of schools by Robert Bridges. London: Longmans, Green & Company, 1924. McKay 132.

> No markings.

10. *New Verse Written in 1921.* Oxford: Clarendon Press, 1925. McKay 67a.

> Inserted card: 'With the compliments of the Delegates of the Clarendon Press, Oxford.' No markings.

11. *The Testament of Beauty.* Oxford: Clarendon Press, 1929. McKay 71a.

> Inscribed 'William Butler Yeats from Robert Bridges.' Pages uncut.

12. *Poems of Gerard Manley Hopkins.* Edited with notes by Robert Bridges. Second edition, with an appendix of additional poems, and a critical introduction by Charles Williams. London: Oxford University Press, 1930. No. 14 of the 250 copies on hand made paper. Not in McKay.

> 'The Leaden Echo' marked in the Contents.

Index